ROSINSKI - VAN HA[...]

THORGAL

The Invisible Fortress

Colour work: GRAZA

9th CINEBOOK
The 9th Art Publisher

Original title: Thorgal 19 – La forteresse invisible

Original edition: © Rosinski & Van Hamme, 1993, Editions du Lombard
(Dargaud-Lombard SA)
www.lelombard.com
All rights reserved

English translation: © 2011 Cinebook Ltd

Translator: Jerome Saincantin
Lettering and text layout: Imadjinn
Printed in Spain by Just Colour Graphic

This edition first published in Great Britain in 2011 by
Cinebook Ltd
56 Beech Avenue
Canterbury, Kent
CT4 7TA
www.cinebook.com

A CIP catalogue record for this book
is available from the British Library

ISBN 978-1-84918-103-7

9th CINEBOOK
The 9th Art Publisher

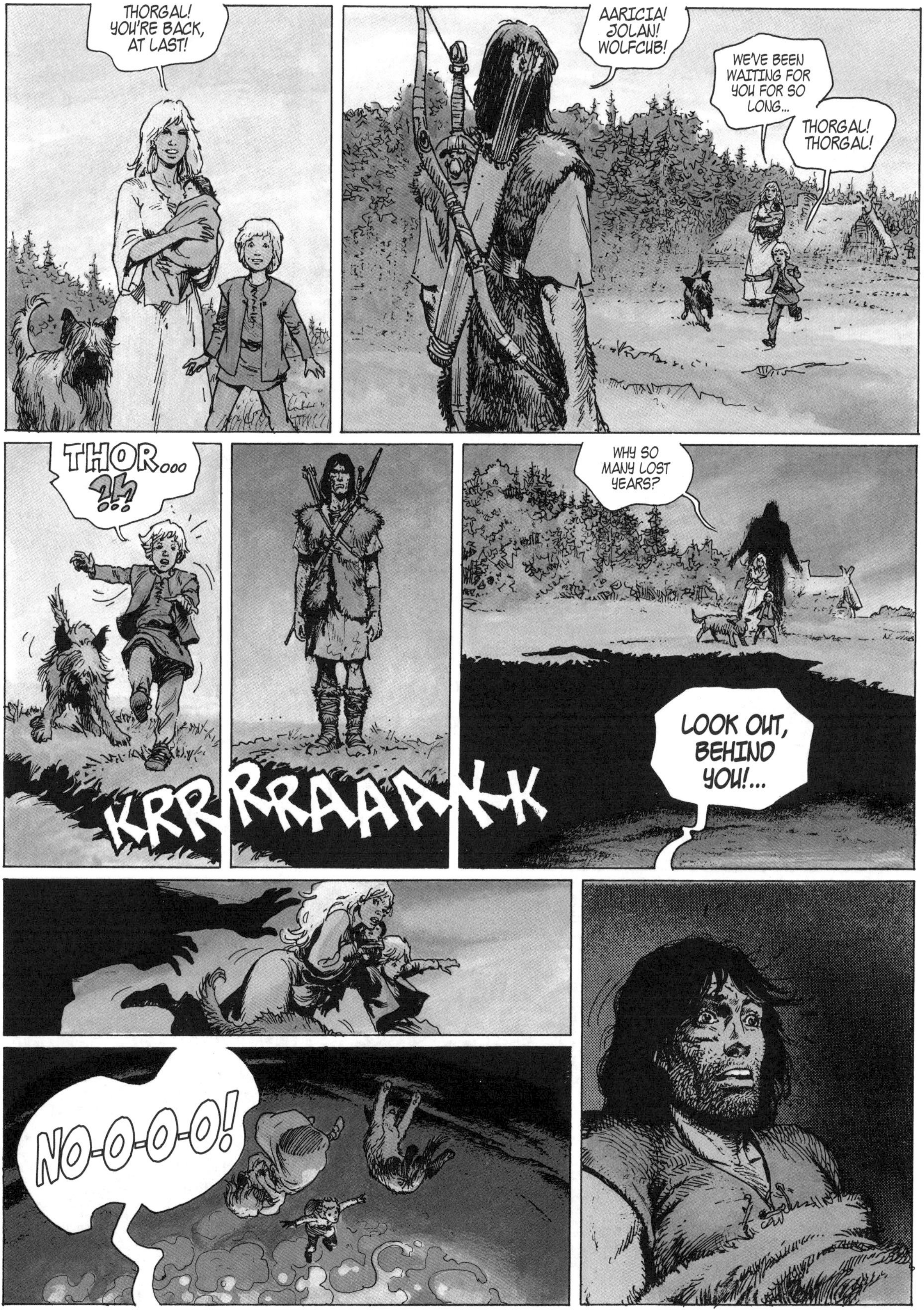
THORGAL! YOU'RE BACK, AT LAST!
AARICIA! JOLAN! WOLFCUB!
WE'VE BEEN WAITING FOR YOU FOR SO LONG...
THORGAL! THORGAL!
THOR...?!
WHY SO MANY LOST YEARS?
LOOK OUT, BEHIND YOU!...
KRRRRAAAKK
NO-O-O-O!

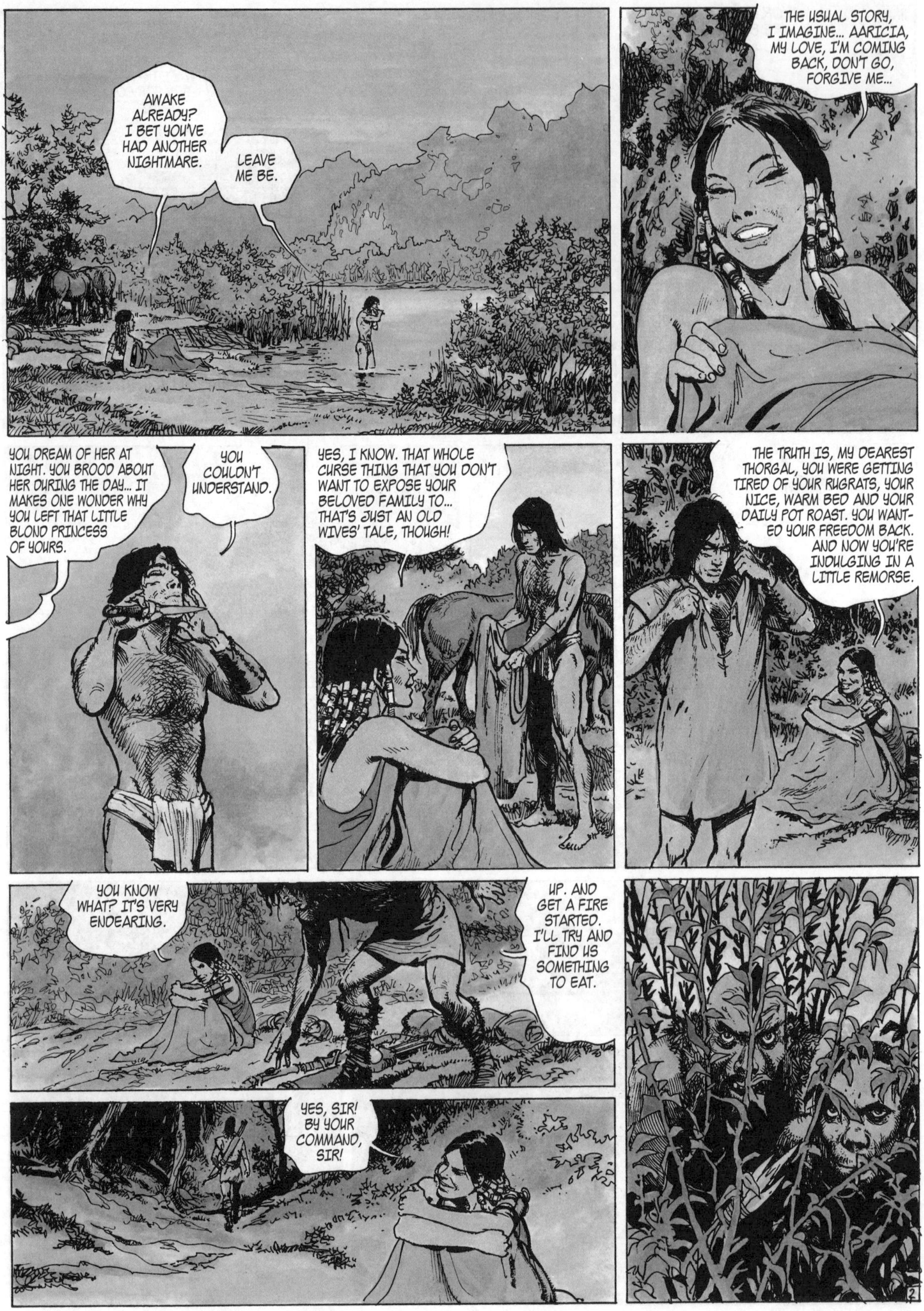
AWAKE ALREADY? I BET YOU'VE HAD ANOTHER NIGHTMARE.
LEAVE ME BE.
THE USUAL STORY, I IMAGINE... AARICIA, MY LOVE, I'M COMING BACK, DON'T GO, FORGIVE ME...
YOU DREAM OF HER AT NIGHT. YOU BROOD ABOUT HER DURING THE DAY... IT MAKES ONE WONDER WHY YOU LEFT THAT LITTLE BLOND PRINCESS OF YOURS.
YOU COULDN'T UNDERSTAND.
YES, I KNOW. THAT WHOLE CURSE THING THAT YOU DON'T WANT TO EXPOSE YOUR BELOVED FAMILY TO... THAT'S JUST AN OLD WIVES' TALE, THOUGH!
THE TRUTH IS, MY DEAREST THORGAL, YOU WERE GETTING TIRED OF YOUR RUGRATS, YOUR NICE, WARM BED AND YOUR DAILY POT ROAST. YOU WANTED YOUR FREEDOM BACK. AND NOW YOU'RE INDULGING IN A LITTLE REMORSE.
YOU KNOW WHAT? IT'S VERY ENDEARING.
UP. AND GET A FIRE STARTED. I'LL TRY AND FIND US SOMETHING TO EAT.
YES, SIR! BY YOUR COMMAND, SIR!
2

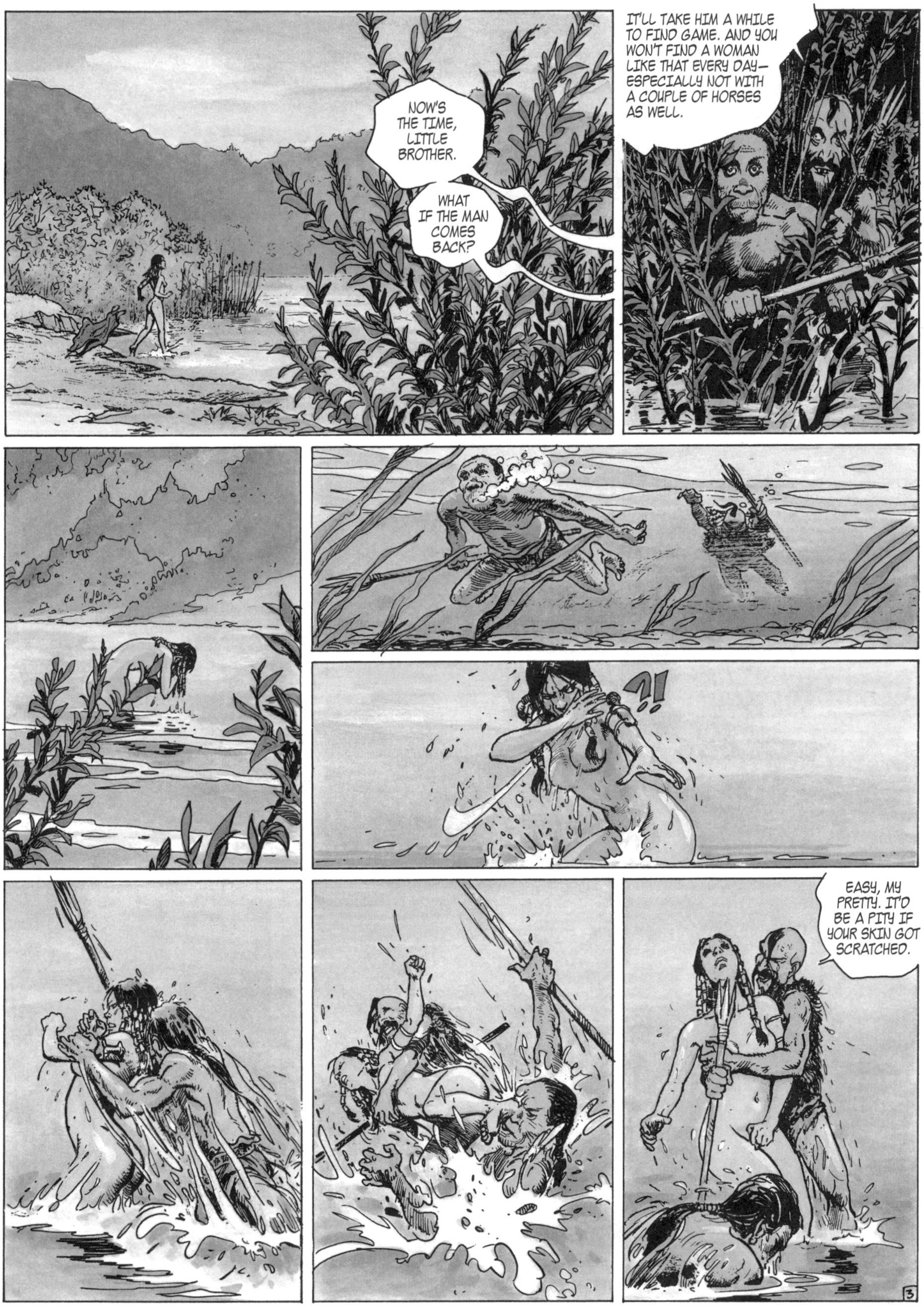
NOW'S THE TIME, LITTLE BROTHER.
WHAT IF THE MAN COMES BACK?
IT'LL TAKE HIM A WHILE TO FIND GAME. AND YOU WON'T FIND A WOMAN LIKE THAT EVERY DAY— ESPECIALLY NOT WITH A COUPLE OF HORSES AS WELL.
?!
EASY, MY PRETTY. IT'D BE A PITY IF YOUR SKIN GOT SCRATCHED.
3

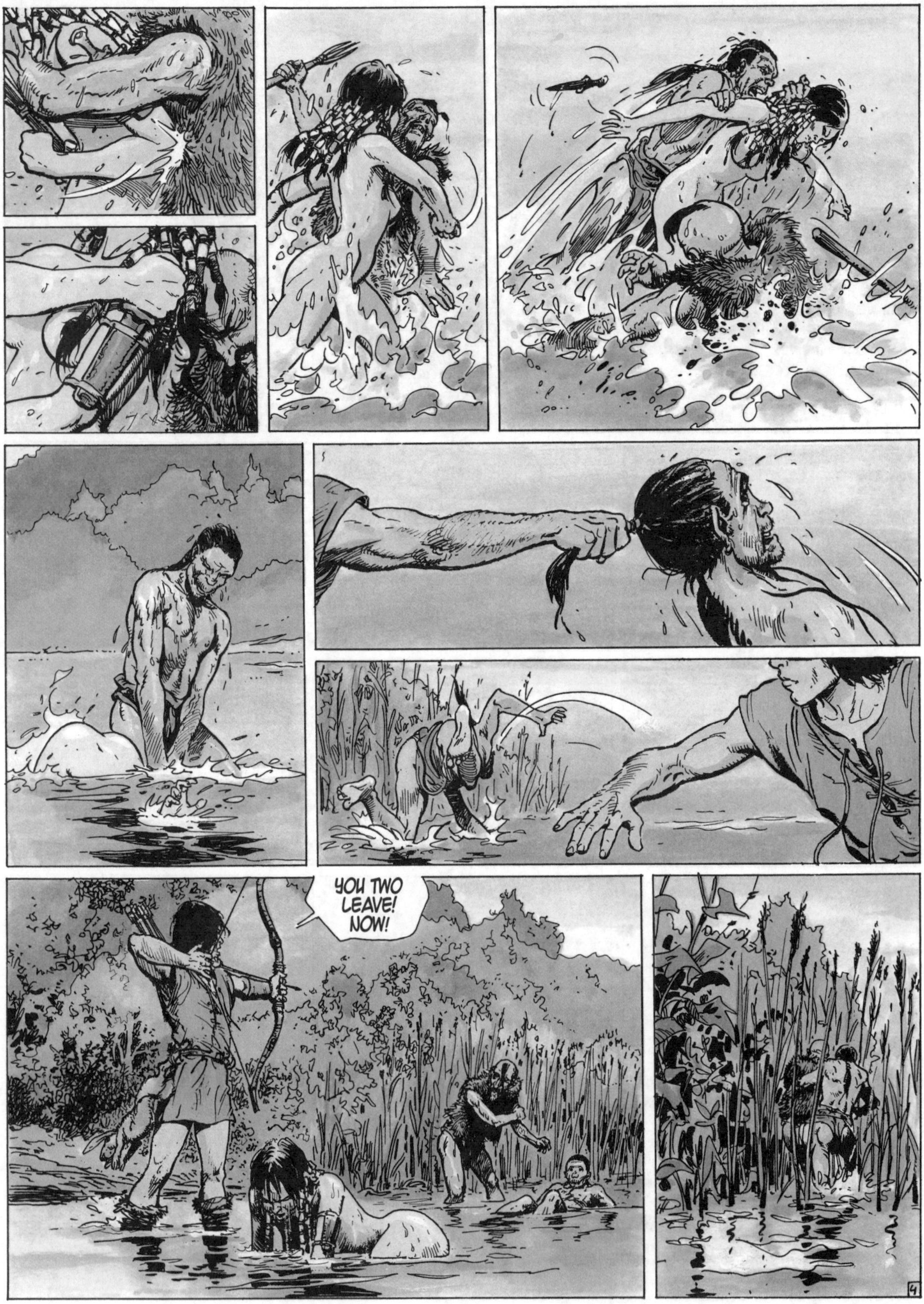
YOU TWO LEAVE! NOW!
4

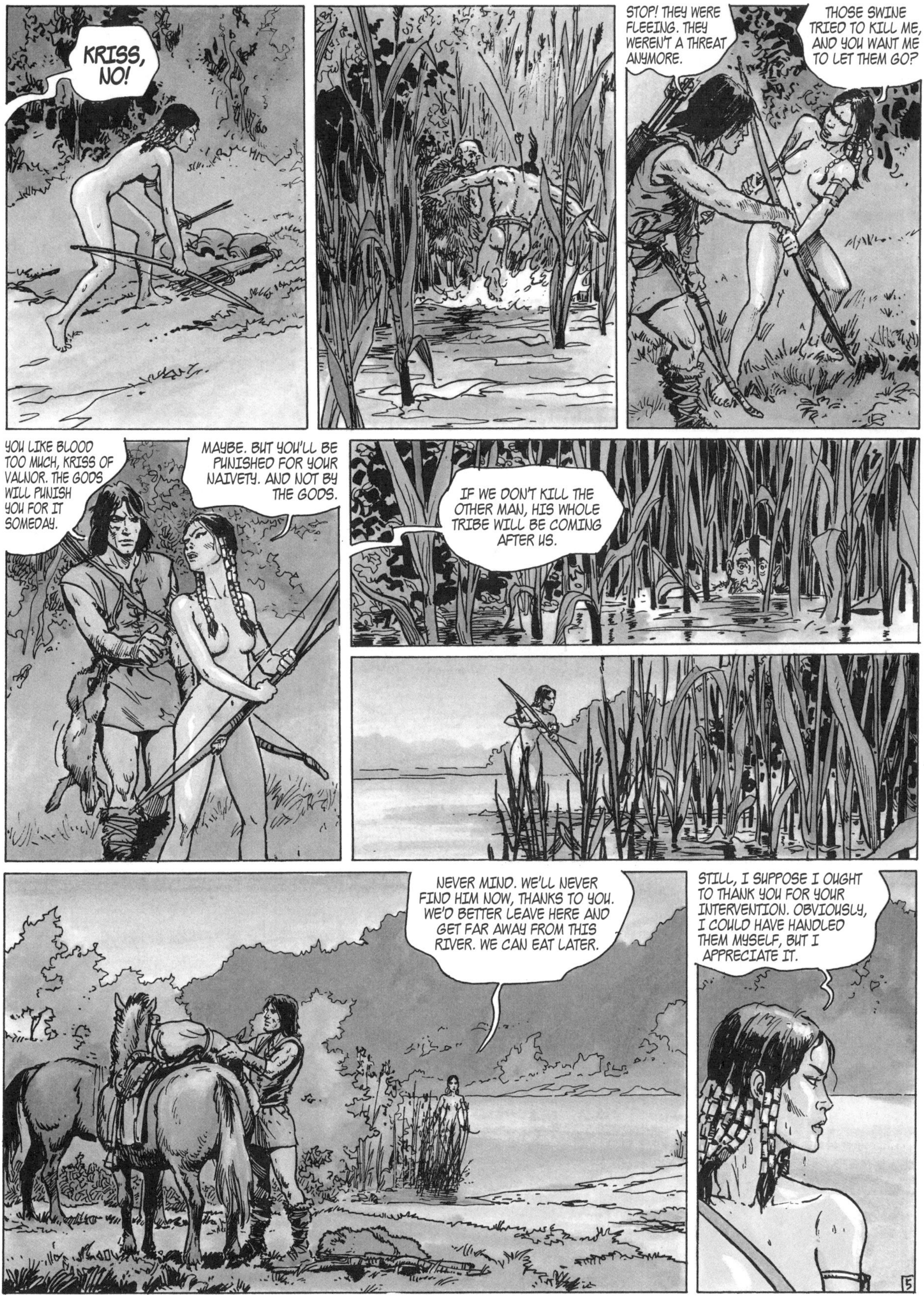
KRISS, NO!
STOP! THEY WERE FLEEING. THEY WEREN'T A THREAT ANYMORE.
THOSE SWINE TRIED TO KILL ME, AND YOU WANT ME TO LET THEM GO?
YOU LIKE BLOOD TOO MUCH, KRISS OF VALNOR. THE GODS WILL PUNISH YOU FOR IT SOMEDAY.
MAYBE. BUT YOU'LL BE PUNISHED FOR YOUR NAIVETY. AND NOT BY THE GODS.
IF WE DON'T KILL THE OTHER MAN, HIS WHOLE TRIBE WILL BE COMING AFTER US.
NEVER MIND. WE'LL NEVER FIND HIM NOW, THANKS TO YOU. WE'D BETTER LEAVE HERE AND GET FAR AWAY FROM THIS RIVER. WE CAN EAT LATER.
STILL, I SUPPOSE I OUGHT TO THANK YOU FOR YOUR INTERVENTION. OBVIOUSLY, I COULD HAVE HANDLED THEM MYSELF, BUT I APPRECIATE IT.
5

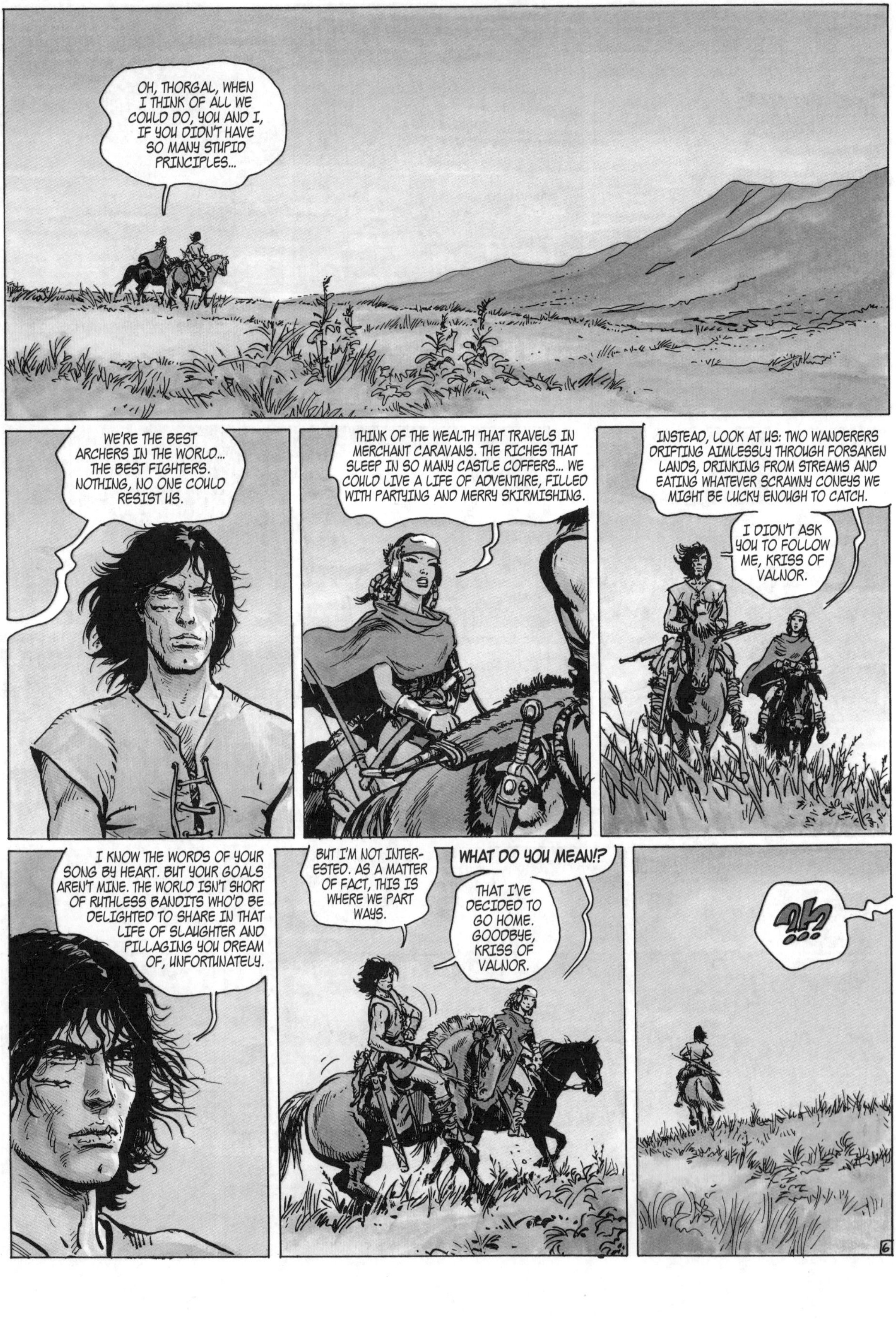
OH, THORGAL, WHEN I THINK OF ALL WE COULD DO, YOU AND I, IF YOU DIDN'T HAVE SO MANY STUPID PRINCIPLES...
WE'RE THE BEST ARCHERS IN THE WORLD... THE BEST FIGHTERS. NOTHING, NO ONE COULD RESIST US.
THINK OF THE WEALTH THAT TRAVELS IN MERCHANT CARAVANS. THE RICHES THAT SLEEP IN SO MANY CASTLE COFFERS... WE COULD LIVE A LIFE OF ADVENTURE, FILLED WITH PARTYING AND MERRY SKIRMISHING.
INSTEAD, LOOK AT US: TWO WANDERERS DRIFTING AIMLESSLY THROUGH FORSAKEN LANDS, DRINKING FROM STREAMS AND EATING WHATEVER SCRAWNY CONEYS WE MIGHT BE LUCKY ENOUGH TO CATCH.
I DIDN'T ASK YOU TO FOLLOW ME, KRISS OF VALNOR.
I KNOW THE WORDS OF YOUR SONG BY HEART. BUT YOUR GOALS AREN'T MINE. THE WORLD ISN'T SHORT OF RUTHLESS BANDITS WHO'D BE DELIGHTED TO SHARE IN THAT LIFE OF SLAUGHTER AND PILLAGING YOU DREAM OF, UNFORTUNATELY.
BUT I'M NOT INTERESTED. AS A MATTER OF FACT, THIS IS WHERE WE PART WAYS.
WHAT DO YOU MEAN!?
THAT I'VE DECIDED TO GO HOME. GOODBYE, KRISS OF VALNOR.
?!?
6

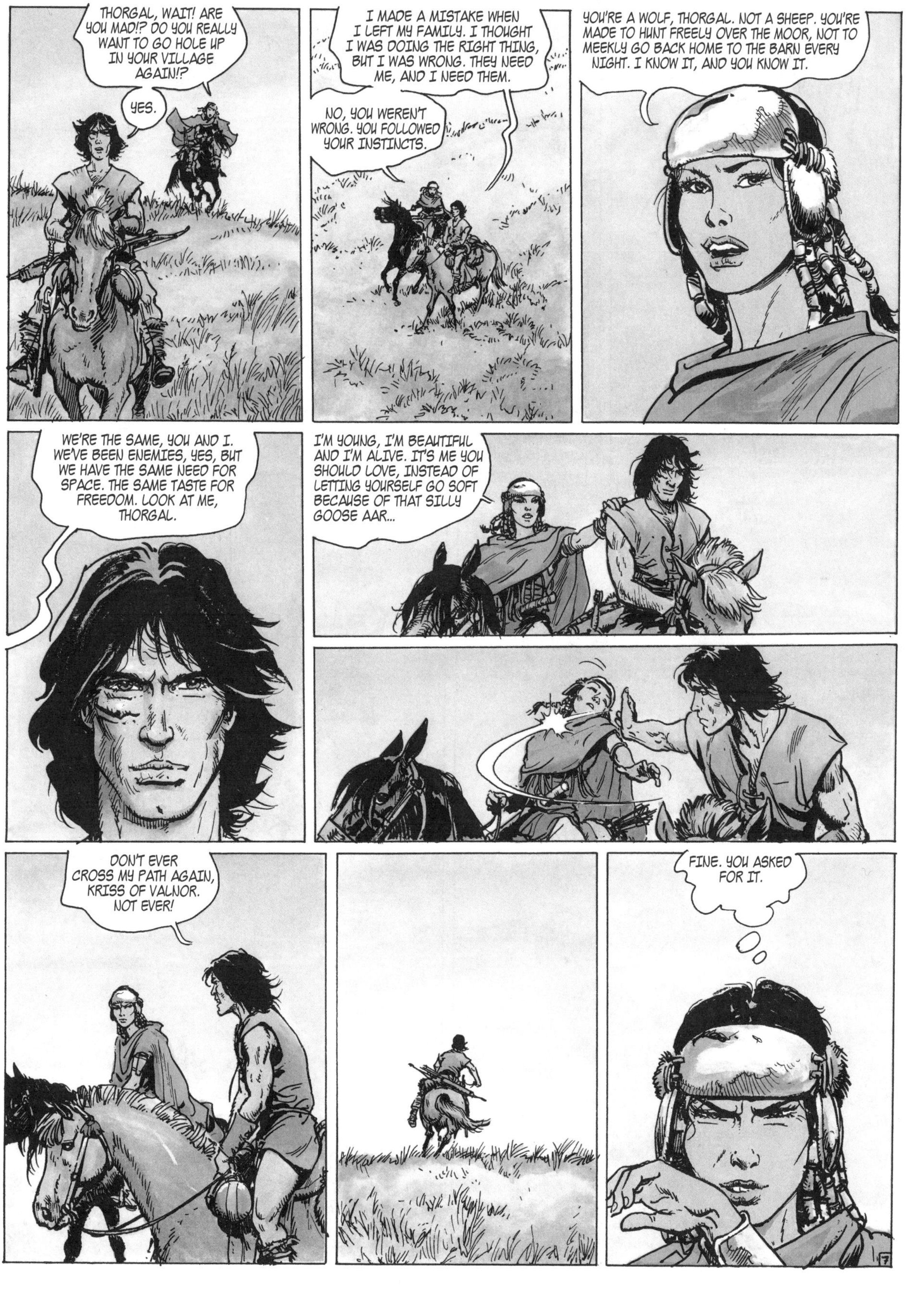
THORGAL, WAIT! ARE YOU MAD!? DO YOU REALLY WANT TO GO HOLE UP IN YOUR VILLAGE AGAIN!?
YES.
I MADE A MISTAKE WHEN I LEFT MY FAMILY. I THOUGHT I WAS DOING THE RIGHT THING, BUT I WAS WRONG. THEY NEED ME, AND I NEED THEM.
NO, YOU WEREN'T WRONG. YOU FOLLOWED YOUR INSTINCTS.
YOU'RE A WOLF, THORGAL. NOT A SHEEP. YOU'RE MADE TO HUNT FREELY OVER THE MOOR, NOT TO MEEKLY GO BACK HOME TO THE BARN EVERY NIGHT. I KNOW IT, AND YOU KNOW IT.
WE'RE THE SAME, YOU AND I. WE'VE BEEN ENEMIES, YES, BUT WE HAVE THE SAME NEED FOR SPACE. THE SAME TASTE FOR FREEDOM. LOOK AT ME, THORGAL.
I'M YOUNG, I'M BEAUTIFUL AND I'M ALIVE. IT'S ME YOU SHOULD LOVE, INSTEAD OF LETTING YOURSELF GO SOFT BECAUSE OF THAT SILLY GOOSE AAR...
DON'T EVER CROSS MY PATH AGAIN, KRISS OF VALNOR. NOT EVER!
FINE. YOU ASKED FOR IT.
7

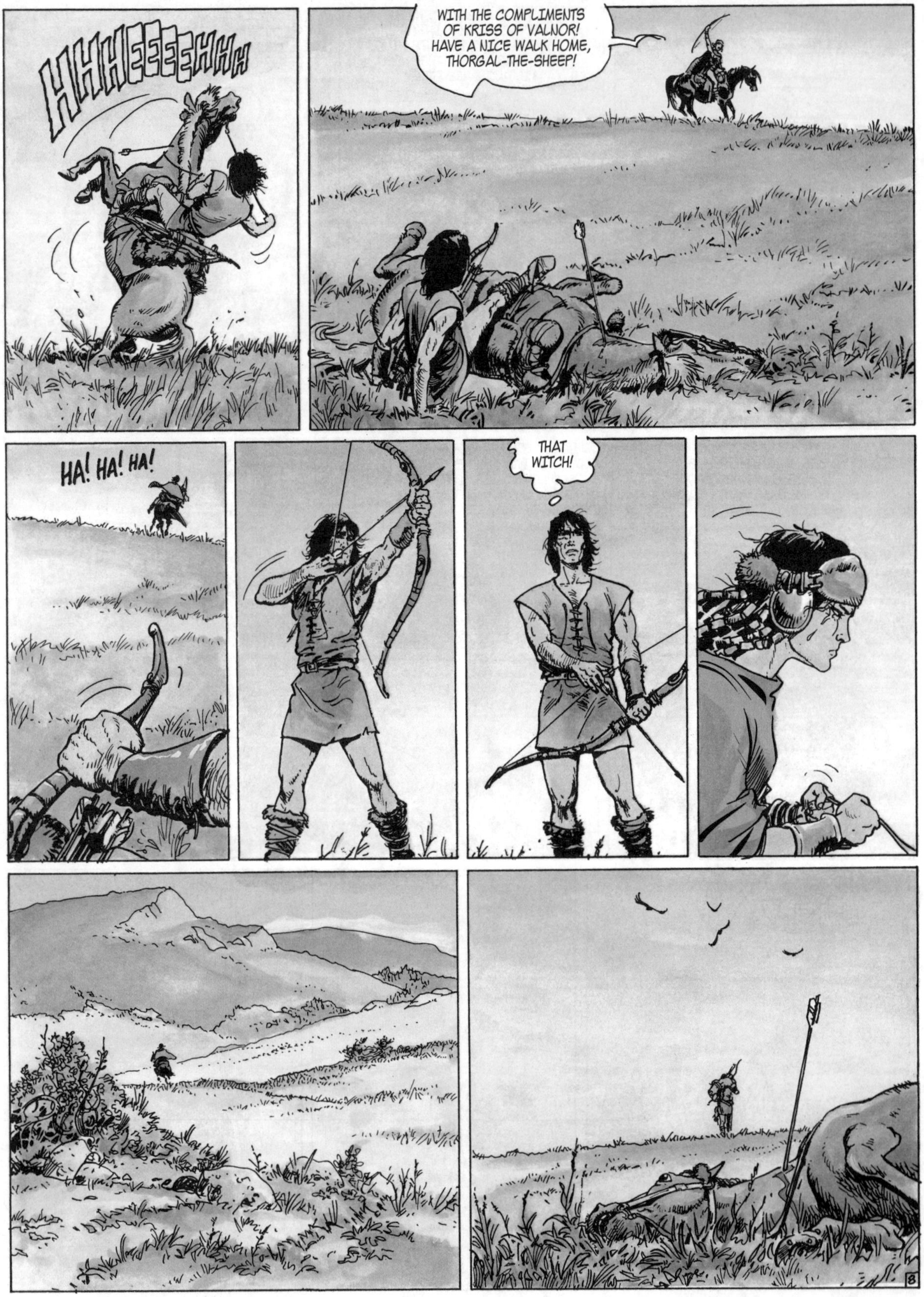
HHHEEEEEHHH
WITH THE COMPLIMENTS OF KRISS OF VALNOR! HAVE A NICE WALK HOME, THORGAL-THE-SHEEP!
HA! HA! HA!
THAT WITCH!
8

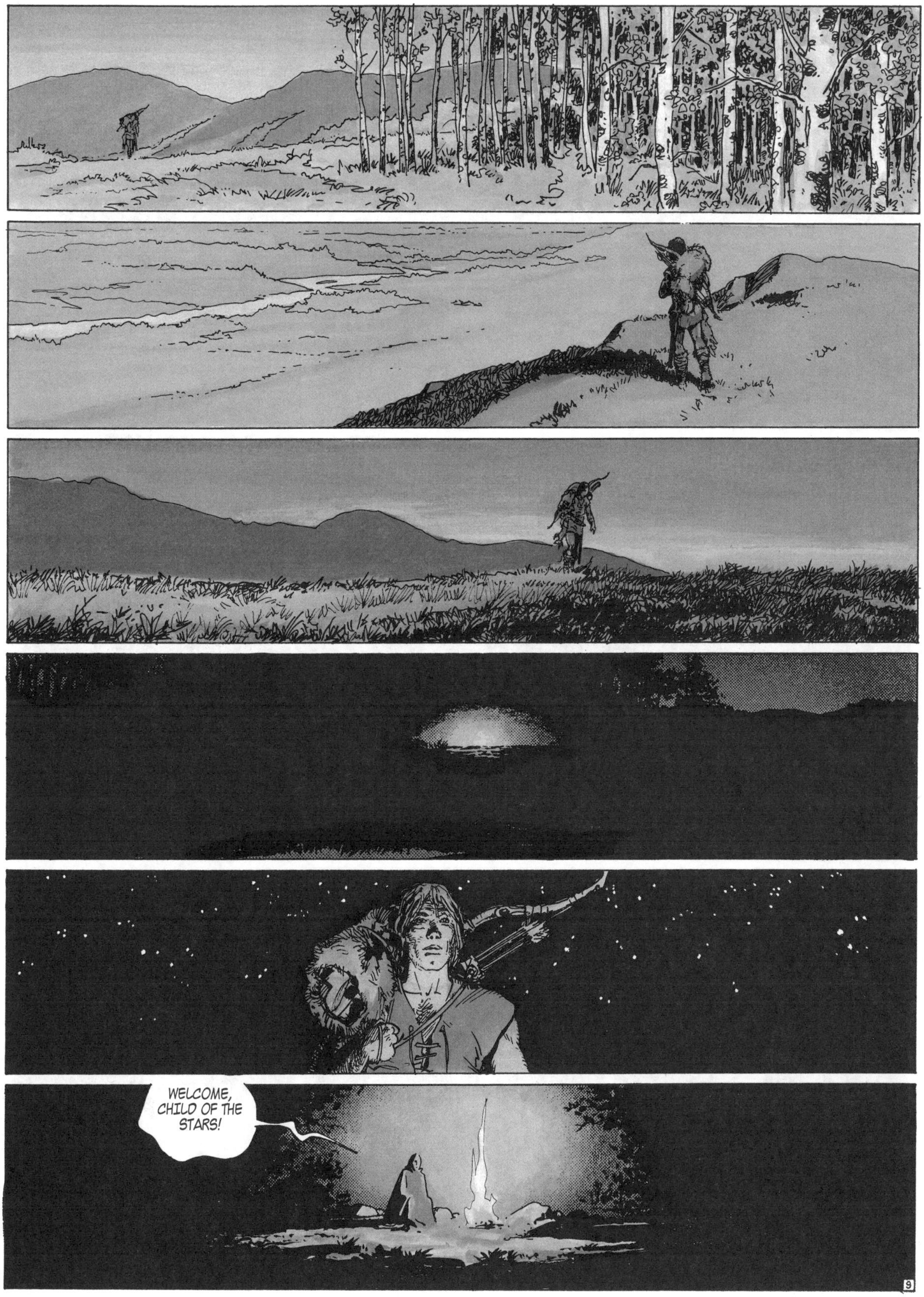
WELCOME, CHILD OF THE STARS!
9

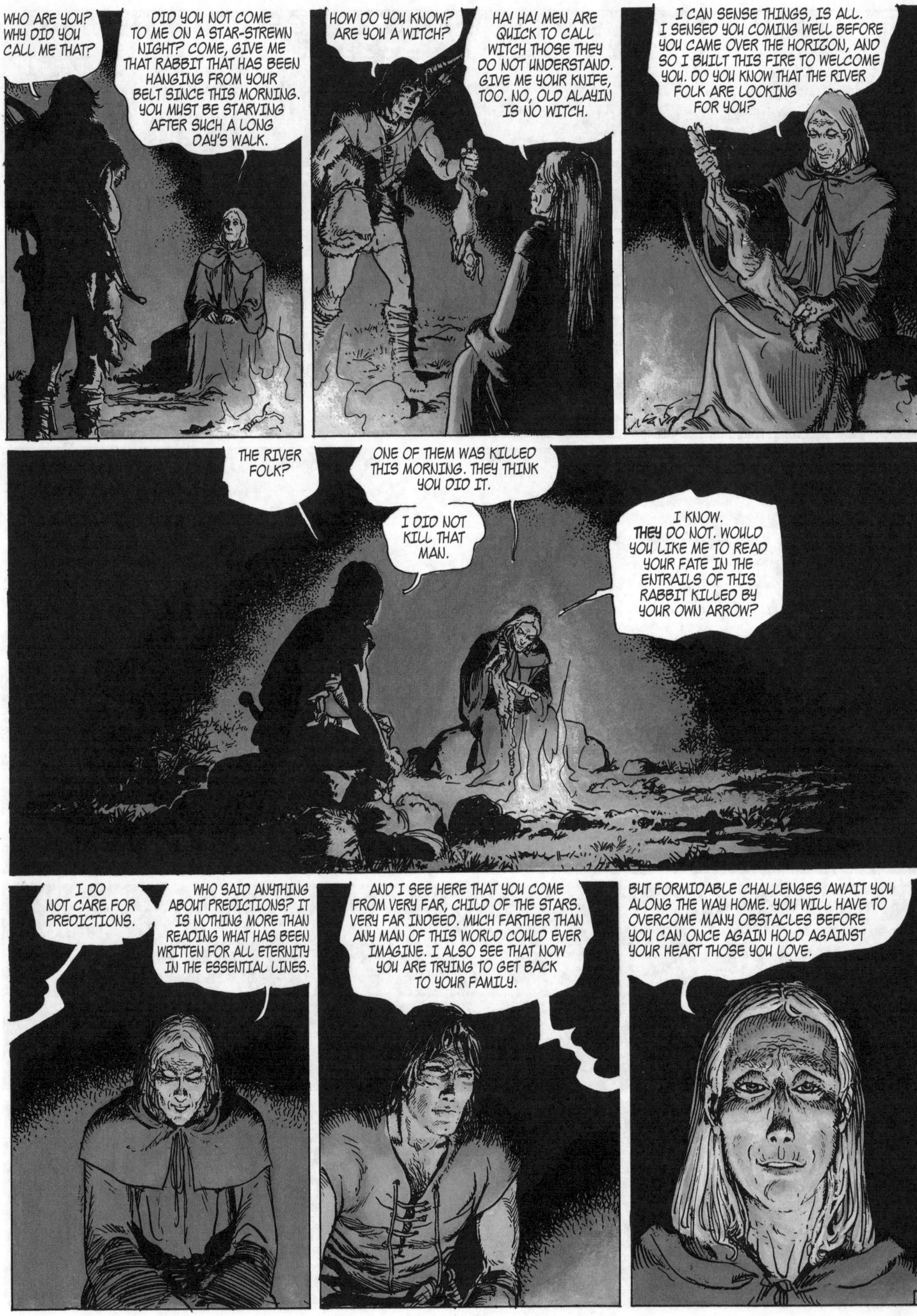
WHO ARE YOU? WHY DID YOU CALL ME THAT?
DID YOU NOT COME TO ME ON A STAR-STREWN NIGHT? COME, GIVE ME THAT RABBIT THAT HAS BEEN HANGING FROM YOUR BELT SINCE THIS MORNING. YOU MUST BE STARVING AFTER SUCH A LONG DAY'S WALK.
HOW DO YOU KNOW? ARE YOU A WITCH?
HA! HA! MEN ARE QUICK TO CALL WITCH THOSE THEY DO NOT UNDERSTAND. GIVE ME YOUR KNIFE, TOO. NO, OLD ALAYIN IS NO WITCH.
I CAN SENSE THINGS, IS ALL. I SENSED YOU COMING WELL BEFORE YOU CAME OVER THE HORIZON, AND SO I BUILT THIS FIRE TO WELCOME YOU. DO YOU KNOW THAT THE RIVER FOLK ARE LOOKING FOR YOU?
THE RIVER FOLK?
ONE OF THEM WAS KILLED THIS MORNING. THEY THINK YOU DID IT.
I DID NOT KILL THAT MAN.
I KNOW. **THEY** DO NOT. WOULD YOU LIKE ME TO READ YOUR FATE IN THE ENTRAILS OF THIS RABBIT KILLED BY YOUR OWN ARROW?
I DO NOT CARE FOR PREDICTIONS.
WHO SAID ANYTHING ABOUT PREDICTIONS? IT IS NOTHING MORE THAN READING WHAT HAS BEEN WRITTEN FOR ALL ETERNITY IN THE ESSENTIAL LINES.
AND I SEE HERE THAT YOU COME FROM VERY FAR, CHILD OF THE STARS. VERY FAR INDEED. MUCH FARTHER THAN ANY MAN OF THIS WORLD COULD EVER IMAGINE. I ALSO SEE THAT NOW YOU ARE TRYING TO GET BACK TO YOUR FAMILY.
BUT FORMIDABLE CHALLENGES AWAIT YOU ALONG THE WAY HOME. YOU WILL HAVE TO OVERCOME MANY OBSTACLES BEFORE YOU CAN ONCE AGAIN HOLD AGAINST YOUR HEART THOSE YOU LOVE.
10

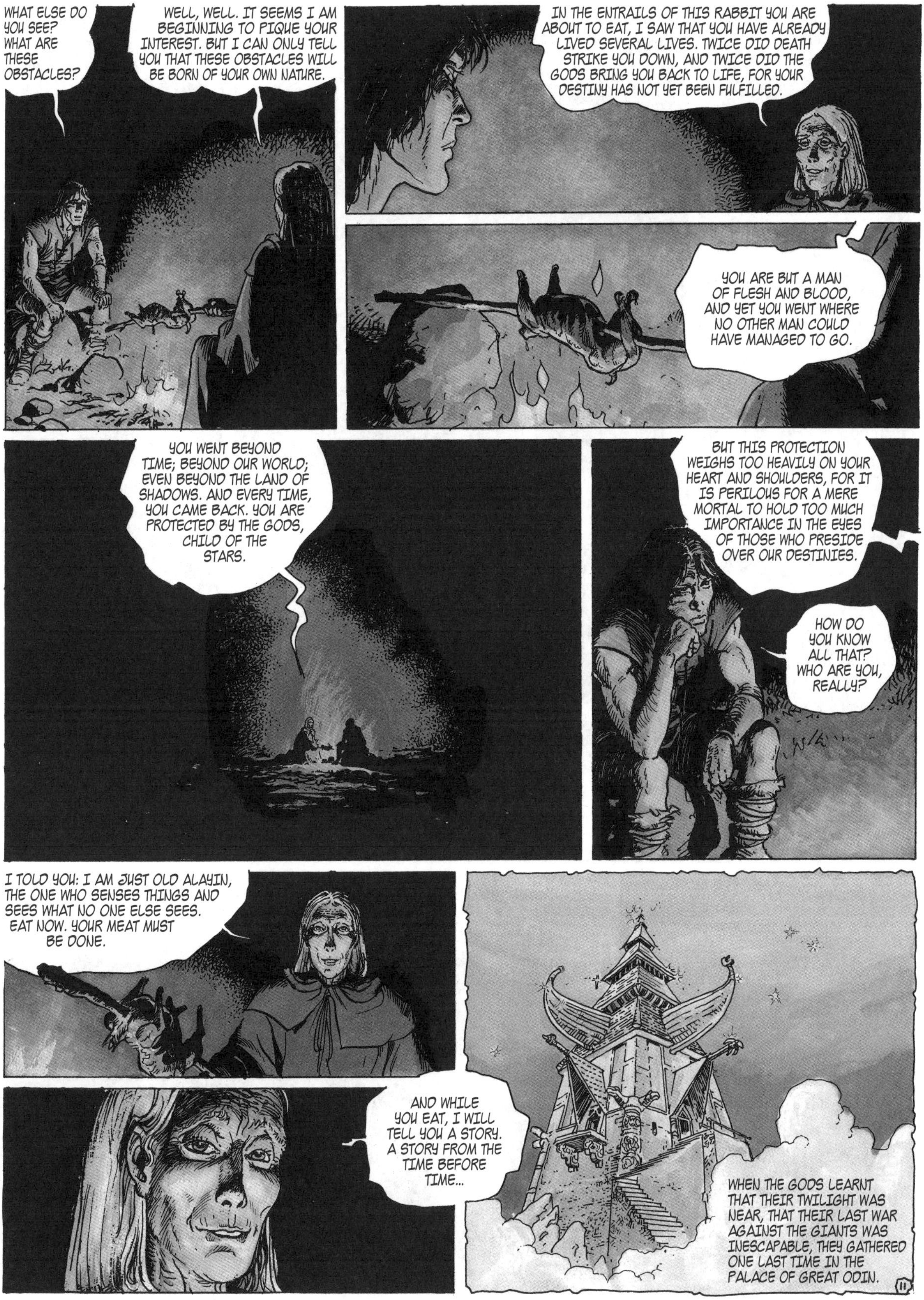

WHAT ELSE DO YOU SEE? WHAT ARE THESE OBSTACLES?
WELL, WELL. IT SEEMS I AM BEGINNING TO PIQUE YOUR INTEREST. BUT I CAN ONLY TELL YOU THAT THESE OBSTACLES WILL BE BORN OF YOUR OWN NATURE.
IN THE ENTRAILS OF THIS RABBIT YOU ARE ABOUT TO EAT, I SAW THAT YOU HAVE ALREADY LIVED SEVERAL LIVES. TWICE DID DEATH STRIKE YOU DOWN, AND TWICE DID THE GODS BRING YOU BACK TO LIFE, FOR YOUR DESTINY HAS NOT YET BEEN FULFILLED.
YOU ARE BUT A MAN OF FLESH AND BLOOD, AND YET YOU WENT WHERE NO OTHER MAN COULD HAVE MANAGED TO GO.
YOU WENT BEYOND TIME; BEYOND OUR WORLD; EVEN BEYOND THE LAND OF SHADOWS. AND EVERY TIME, YOU CAME BACK. YOU ARE PROTECTED BY THE GODS, CHILD OF THE STARS.
BUT THIS PROTECTION WEIGHS TOO HEAVILY ON YOUR HEART AND SHOULDERS, FOR IT IS PERILOUS FOR A MERE MORTAL TO HOLD TOO MUCH IMPORTANCE IN THE EYES OF THOSE WHO PRESIDE OVER OUR DESTINIES.
HOW DO YOU KNOW ALL THAT? WHO ARE YOU, REALLY?
I TOLD YOU: I AM JUST OLD ALAYIN, THE ONE WHO SENSES THINGS AND SEES WHAT NO ONE ELSE SEES. EAT NOW. YOUR MEAT MUST BE DONE.
AND WHILE YOU EAT, I WILL TELL YOU A STORY. A STORY FROM THE TIME BEFORE TIME...
WHEN THE GODS LEARNT THAT THEIR TWILIGHT WAS NEAR, THAT THEIR LAST WAR AGAINST THE GIANTS WAS INESCAPABLE, THEY GATHERED ONE LAST TIME IN THE PALACE OF GREAT ODIN.
11

THERE, ONE AFTER ANOTHER, EVERY GOD AND GODDESS CARVED ON A GRANITE SLAB THE SECRETS OF HIS OR HER POWER AND THE ESSENTIAL LINES OF THE FATES THAT WERE IN THEIR CARE.

ODIN THEN ORDERED THE YOUNGEST OF HIS VALKYRIES, TAIMYR, TO HIDE THE STONE INSIDE AN INVISIBLE FORTRESS, BEYOND TIME AND SPACE. THAT WAY, REGARDLESS OF HOW THE BATTLE ENDED, THE MEMORY OF THE GODS WOULD BE PRESERVED.

THEN, WHILE TAIMYR LEFT TO FULFIL THE MISSION SHE HAD BEEN GIVEN, THE GODS ARMED THEMSELVES FOR THEIR LAST WAR.

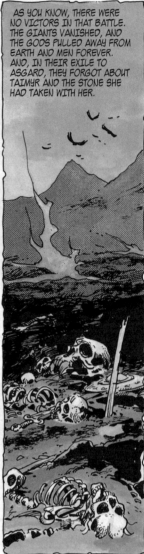

AS YOU KNOW, THERE WERE NO VICTORS IN THAT BATTLE. THE GIANTS VANISHED, AND THE GODS PULLED AWAY FROM EARTH AND MEN FOREVER. AND, IN THEIR EXILE TO ASGARD, THEY FORGOT ABOUT TAIMYR AND THE STONE SHE HAD TAKEN WITH HER.

AND SO IT IS THAT FOR ENDLESS THOUSANDS OF YEARS, A PRISONER AS MUCH AS A GUARDIAN OF HER INVISIBLE FORTRESS, TAIMYR HAS LOOKED AFTER THE SECRET OF THE MEMORY OF THE GODS.

WHY ARE YOU TELLING ME ALL THIS, ALAYIN?

BECAUSE YOUR NAME, LIKE THAT OF MILLIONS OF OTHERS, MUST BE CARVED ON THAT STONE, CHILD OF THE STARS.

ALL YOU WOULD HAVE TO DO IS FIND AND ERASE IT—AND THE GODS WOULD FORGET YOU AT LAST.

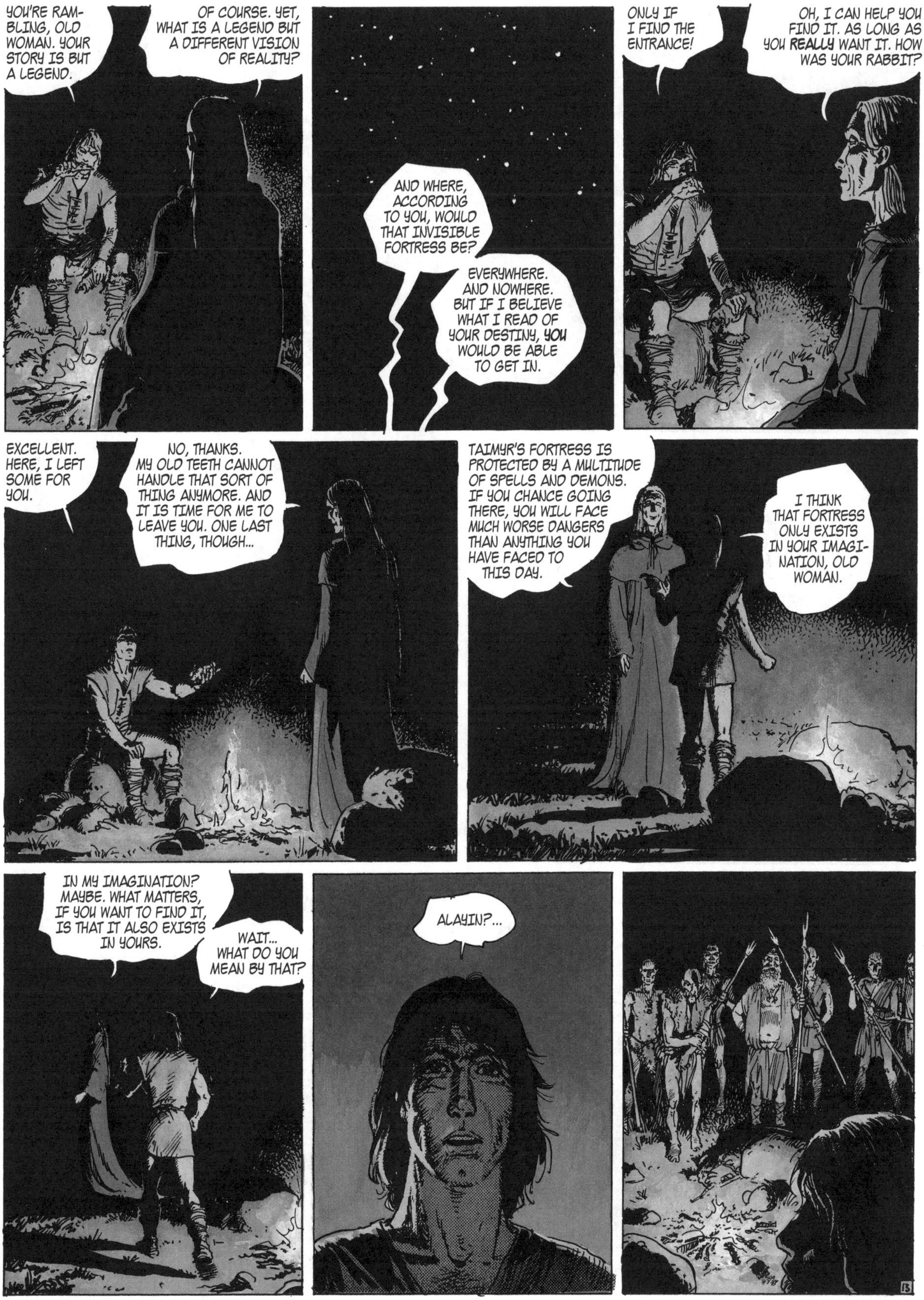
YOU'RE RAMBLING, OLD WOMAN. YOUR STORY IS BUT A LEGEND.
OF COURSE. YET, WHAT IS A LEGEND BUT A DIFFERENT VISION OF REALITY?
AND WHERE, ACCORDING TO YOU, WOULD THAT INVISIBLE FORTRESS BE?
EVERYWHERE. AND NOWHERE. BUT IF I BELIEVE WHAT I READ OF YOUR DESTINY, YOU WOULD BE ABLE TO GET IN.
ONLY IF I FIND THE ENTRANCE!
OH, I CAN HELP YOU FIND IT. AS LONG AS YOU REALLY WANT IT. HOW WAS YOUR RABBIT?
EXCELLENT. HERE, I LEFT SOME FOR YOU.
NO, THANKS. MY OLD TEETH CANNOT HANDLE THAT SORT OF THING ANYMORE. AND IT IS TIME FOR ME TO LEAVE YOU. ONE LAST THING, THOUGH...
TAIMYR'S FORTRESS IS PROTECTED BY A MULTITUDE OF SPELLS AND DEMONS. IF YOU CHANCE GOING THERE, YOU WILL FACE MUCH WORSE DANGERS THAN ANYTHING YOU HAVE FACED TO THIS DAY.
I THINK THAT FORTRESS ONLY EXISTS IN YOUR IMAGINATION, OLD WOMAN.
IN MY IMAGINATION? MAYBE. WHAT MATTERS, IF YOU WANT TO FIND IT, IS THAT IT ALSO EXISTS IN YOURS.
WAIT... WHAT DO YOU MEAN BY THAT?
ALAYIN?...
13

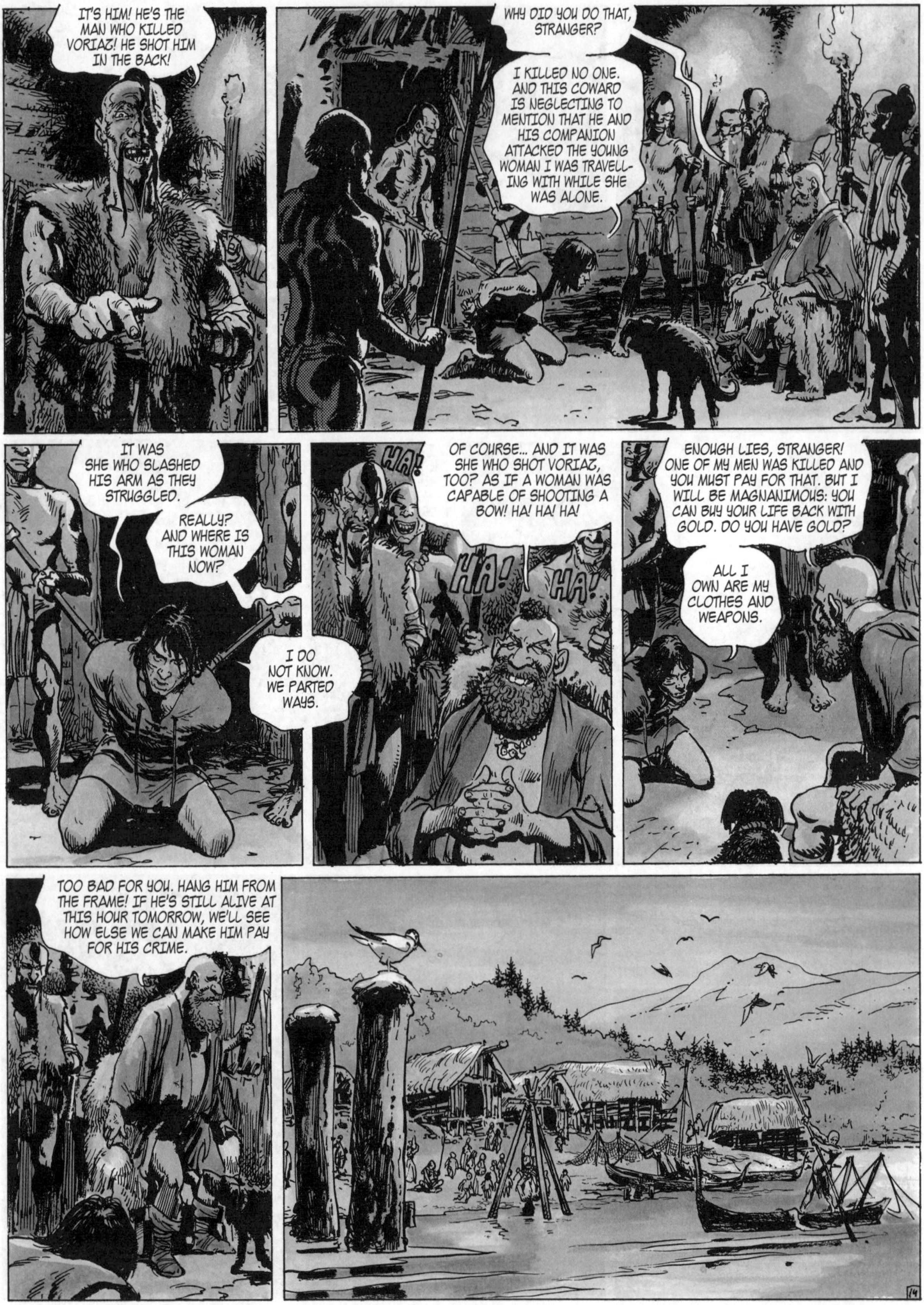
IT'S HIM! HE'S THE MAN WHO KILLED VORIAZ! HE SHOT HIM IN THE BACK!
WHY DID YOU DO THAT, STRANGER?
I KILLED NO ONE. AND THIS COWARD IS NEGLECTING TO MENTION THAT HE AND HIS COMPANION ATTACKED THE YOUNG WOMAN I WAS TRAVELL-ING WITH WHILE SHE WAS ALONE.
IT WAS SHE WHO SLASHED HIS ARM AS THEY STRUGGLED.
REALLY? AND WHERE IS THIS WOMAN NOW?
I DO NOT KNOW. WE PARTED WAYS.
HA!
OF COURSE... AND IT WAS SHE WHO SHOT VORIAZ, TOO? AS IF A WOMAN WAS CAPABLE OF SHOOTING A BOW! HA! HA! HA!
HA!
HA!
ENOUGH LIES, STRANGER! ONE OF MY MEN WAS KILLED AND YOU MUST PAY FOR THAT. BUT I WILL BE MAGNANIMOUS: YOU CAN BUY YOUR LIFE BACK WITH GOLD. DO YOU HAVE GOLD?
ALL I OWN ARE MY CLOTHES AND WEAPONS.
TOO BAD FOR YOU. HANG HIM FROM THE FRAME! IF HE'S STILL ALIVE AT THIS HOUR TOMORROW, WE'LL SEE HOW ELSE WE CAN MAKE HIM PAY FOR HIS CRIME.
14

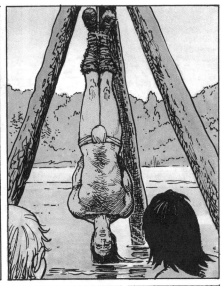

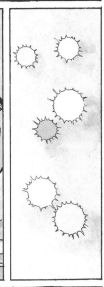

WELL, MY BOY. WHAT UNPLEASANT SITUATION HAVE YOU GOT YOURSELF INTO?

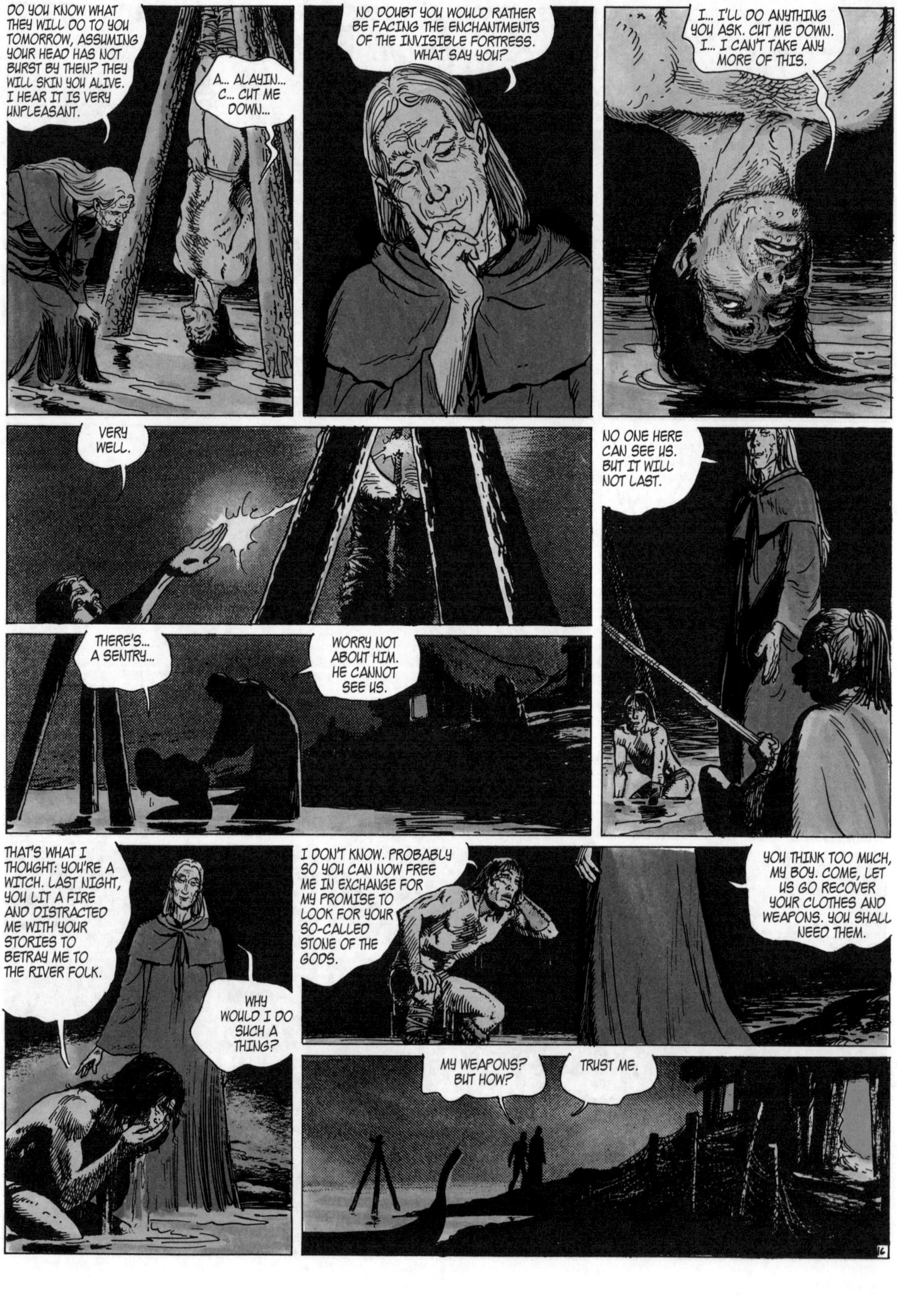

DO YOU KNOW WHAT THEY WILL DO TO YOU TOMORROW, ASSUMING YOUR HEAD HAS NOT BURST BY THEN? THEY WILL SKIN YOU ALIVE. I HEAR IT IS VERY UNPLEASANT.
A... ALAYIN... C... CUT ME DOWN...
NO DOUBT YOU WOULD RATHER BE FACING THE ENCHANTMENTS OF THE INVISIBLE FORTRESS. WHAT SAY YOU?
I... I'LL DO ANYTHING YOU ASK. CUT ME DOWN. I... I CAN'T TAKE ANY MORE OF THIS.
VERY WELL.
THERE'S... A SENTRY...
WORRY NOT ABOUT HIM. HE CANNOT SEE US.
NO ONE HERE CAN SEE US. BUT IT WILL NOT LAST.
THAT'S WHAT I THOUGHT: YOU'RE A WITCH. LAST NIGHT, YOU LIT A FIRE AND DISTRACTED ME WITH YOUR STORIES TO BETRAY ME TO THE RIVER FOLK.
WHY WOULD I DO SUCH A THING?
I DON'T KNOW. PROBABLY SO YOU CAN NOW FREE ME IN EXCHANGE FOR MY PROMISE TO LOOK FOR YOUR SO-CALLED STONE OF THE GODS.
YOU THINK TOO MUCH, MY BOY. COME, LET US GO RECOVER YOUR CLOTHES AND WEAPONS. YOU SHALL NEED THEM.
MY WEAPONS? BUT HOW?
TRUST ME.
16

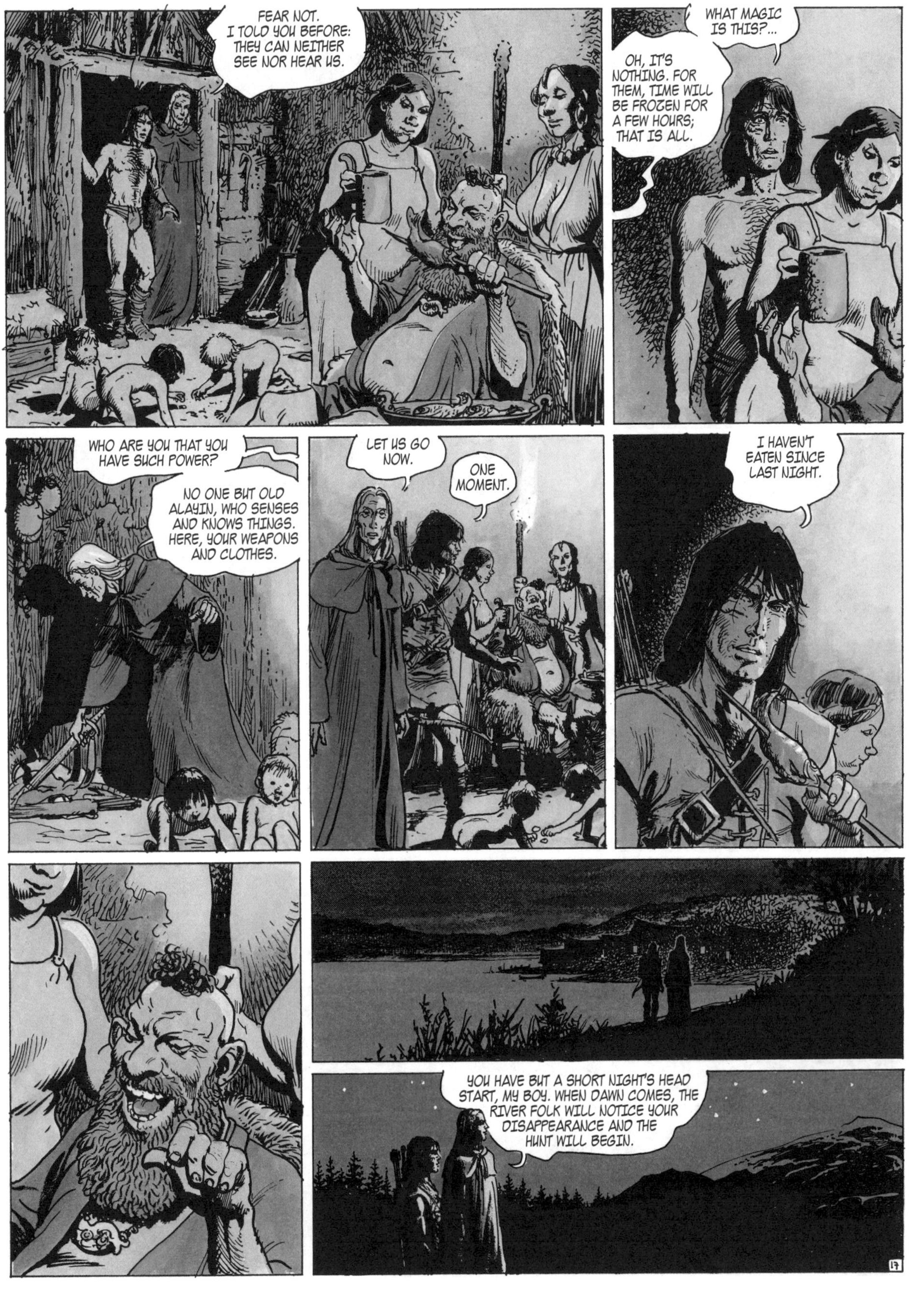
FEAR NOT. I TOLD YOU BEFORE: THEY CAN NEITHER SEE NOR HEAR US.
WHAT MAGIC IS THIS?...
OH, IT'S NOTHING. FOR THEM, TIME WILL BE FROZEN FOR A FEW HOURS; THAT IS ALL.
WHO ARE YOU THAT YOU HAVE SUCH POWER?
NO ONE BUT OLD ALAYIN, WHO SENSES AND KNOWS THINGS. HERE, YOUR WEAPONS AND CLOTHES.
LET US GO NOW.
ONE MOMENT.
I HAVEN'T EATEN SINCE LAST NIGHT.
YOU HAVE BUT A SHORT NIGHT'S HEAD START, MY BOY. WHEN DAWN COMES, THE RIVER FOLK WILL NOTICE YOUR DISAPPEARANCE AND THE HUNT WILL BEGIN.
17

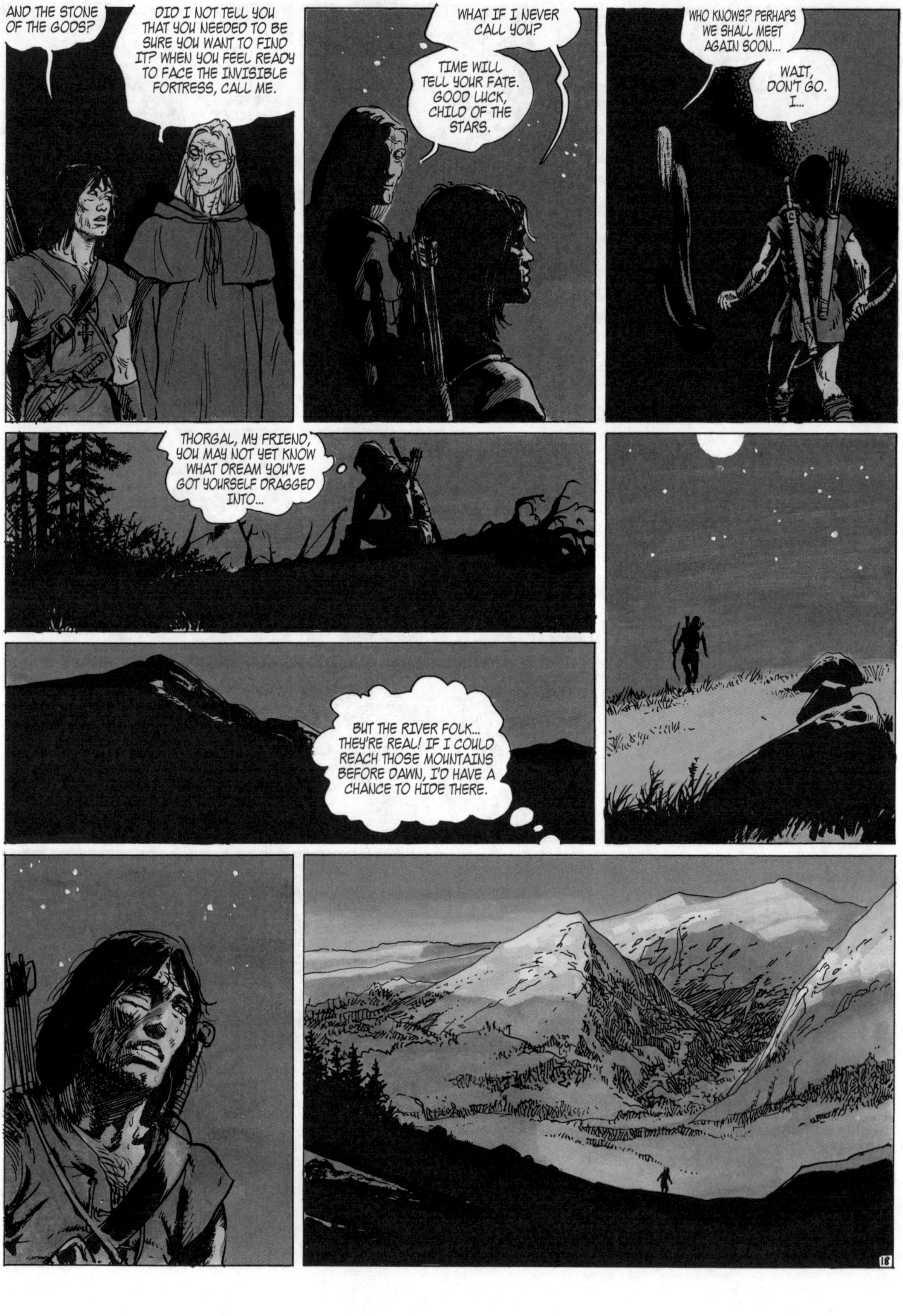
AND THE STONE OF THE GODS?
DID I NOT TELL YOU THAT YOU NEEDED TO BE SURE YOU WANT TO FIND IT? WHEN YOU FEEL READY TO FACE THE INVISIBLE FORTRESS, CALL ME.
WHAT IF I NEVER CALL YOU?
TIME WILL TELL YOUR FATE. GOOD LUCK, CHILD OF THE STARS.
WHO KNOWS? PERHAPS WE SHALL MEET AGAIN SOON...
WAIT, DON'T GO. I...
THORGAL, MY FRIEND, YOU MAY NOT YET KNOW WHAT DREAM YOU'VE GOT YOURSELF DRAGGED INTO...
BUT THE RIVER FOLK... THEY'RE REAL! IF I COULD REACH THOSE MOUNTAINS BEFORE DAWN, I'D HAVE A CHANCE TO HIDE THERE.
18

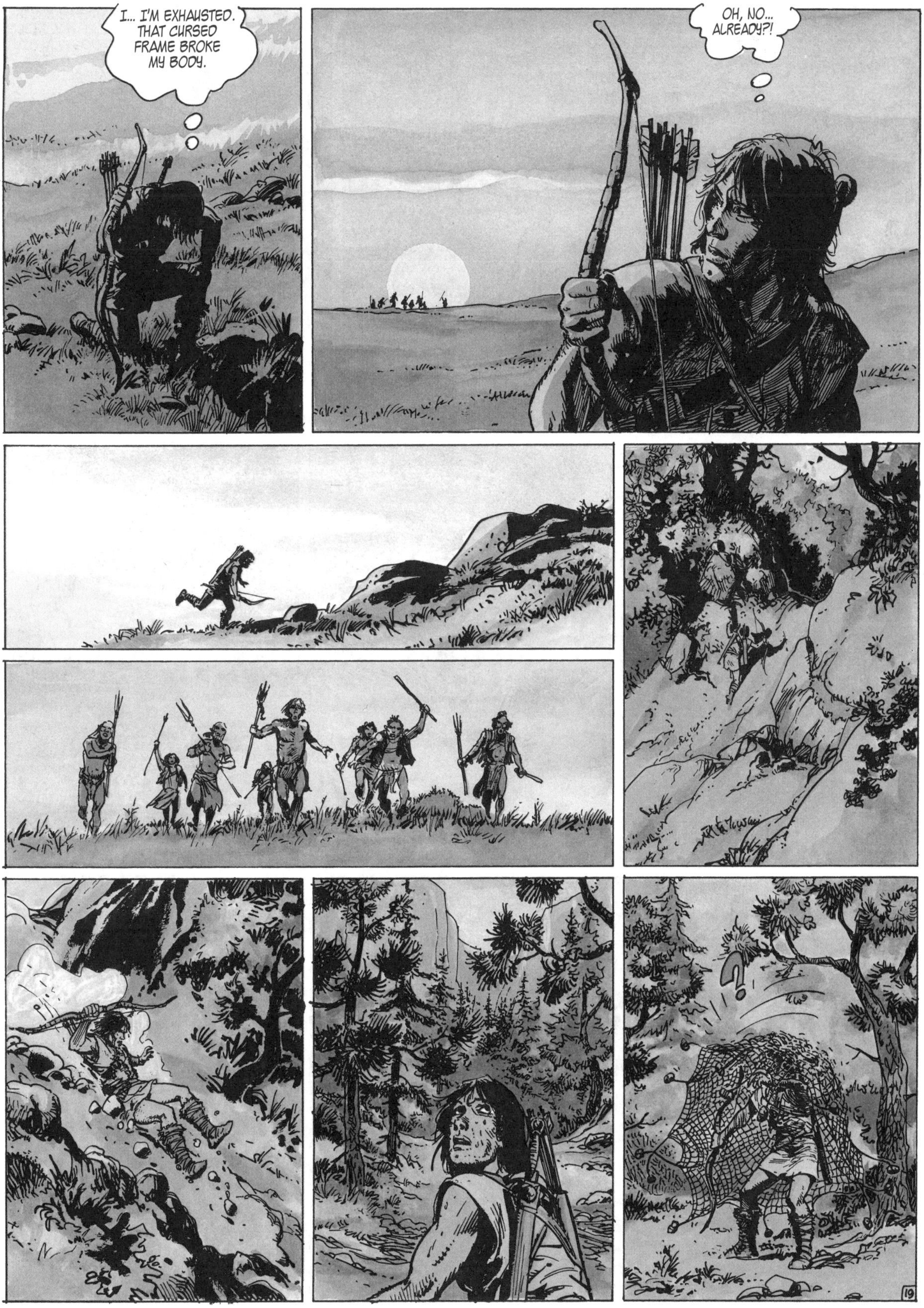
I... I'M EXHAUSTED. THAT CURSED FRAME BROKE MY BODY.
OH, NO... ALREADY?!
?
19

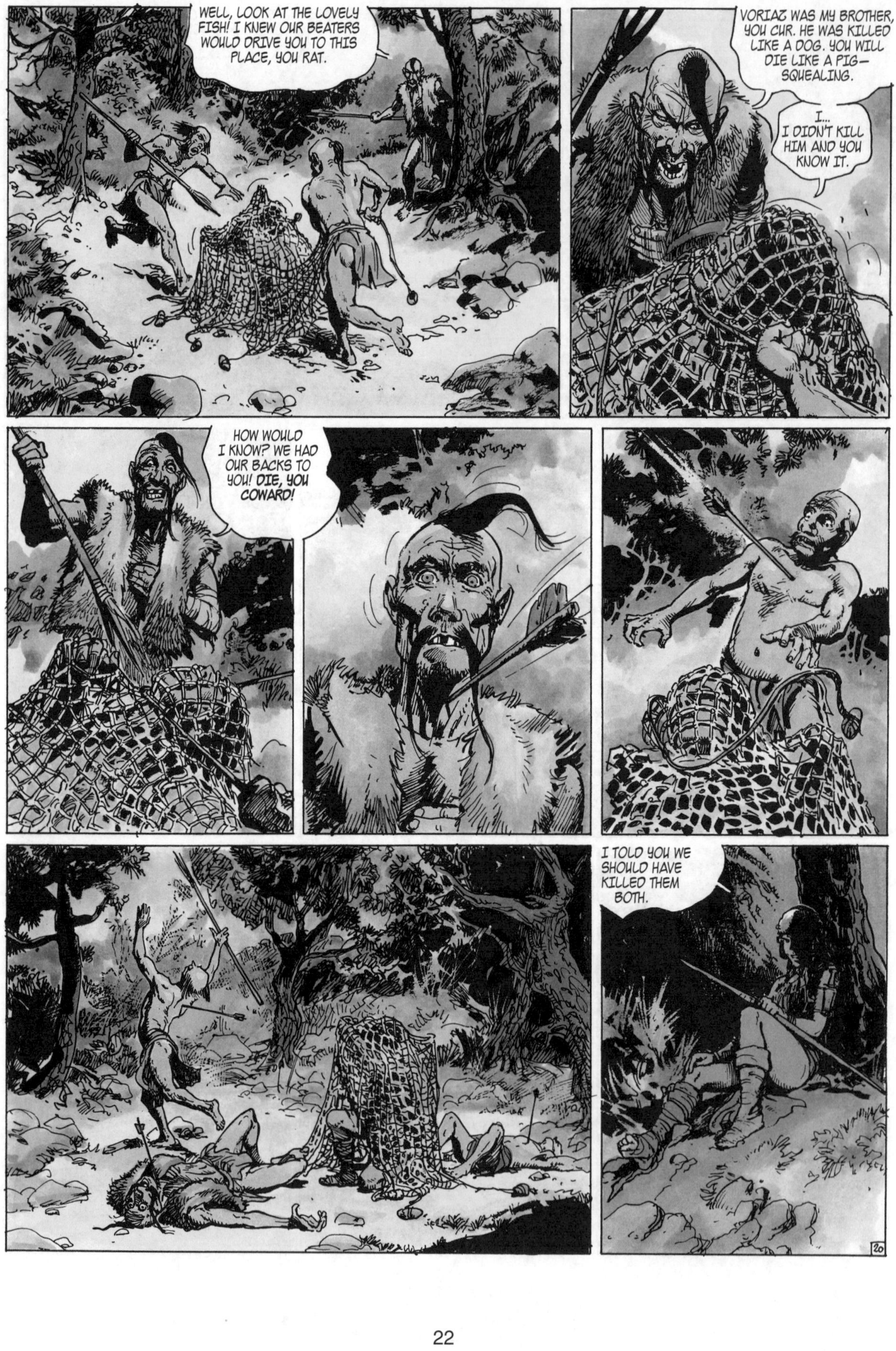
WELL, LOOK AT THE LOVELY FISH! I KNEW OUR BEATERS WOULD DRIVE YOU TO THIS PLACE, YOU RAT.
VORIAZ WAS MY BROTHER, YOU CUR. HE WAS KILLED LIKE A DOG. YOU WILL DIE LIKE A PIG— SQUEALING.
I... I DIDN'T KILL HIM AND YOU KNOW IT.
HOW WOULD I KNOW? WE HAD OUR BACKS TO YOU! DIE, YOU COWARD!
I TOLD YOU WE SHOULD HAVE KILLED THEM BOTH.
20

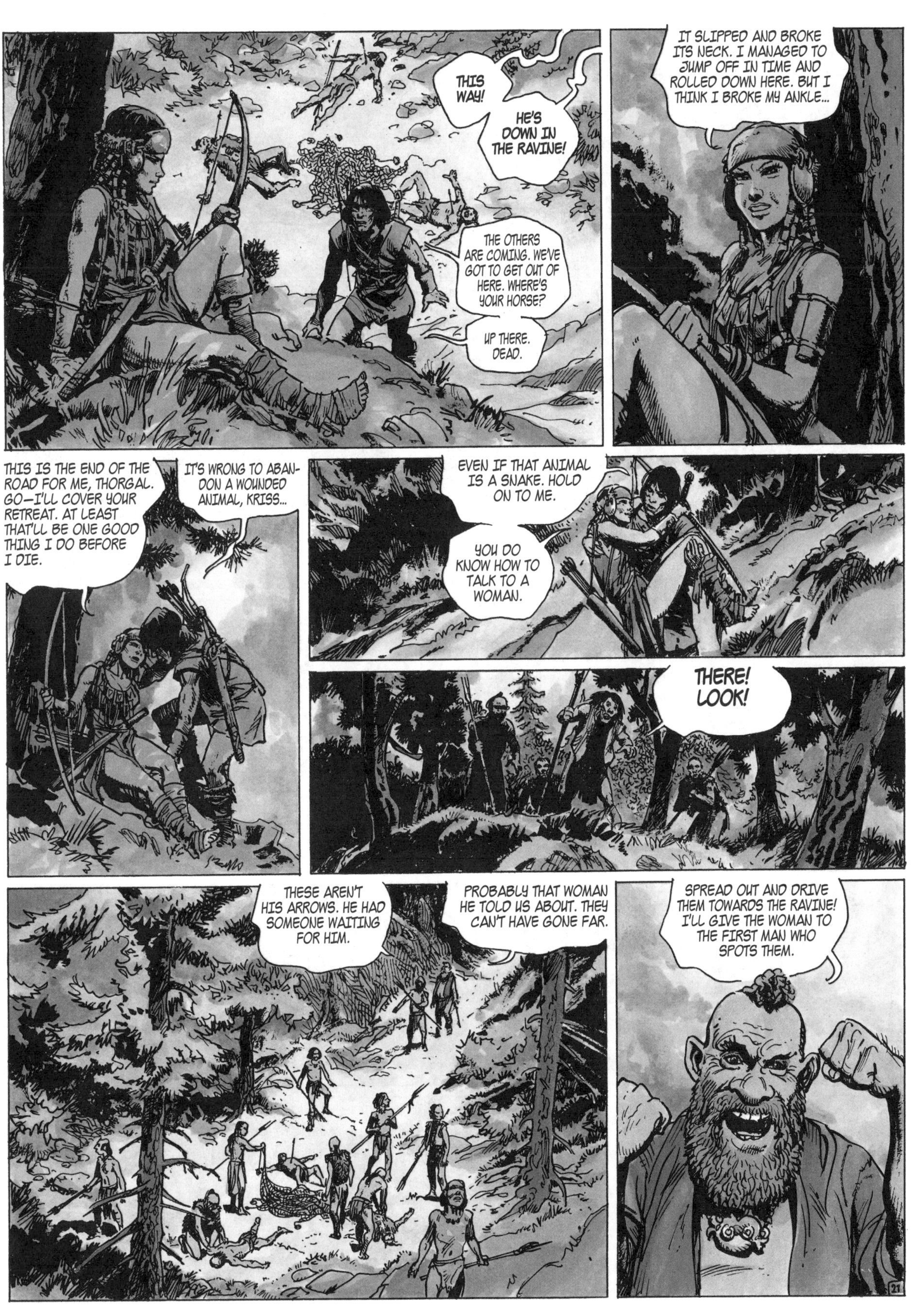
THIS WAY!
HE'S DOWN IN THE RAVINE!
THE OTHERS ARE COMING. WE'VE GOT TO GET OUT OF HERE. WHERE'S YOUR HORSE?
UP THERE. DEAD.
IT SLIPPED AND BROKE ITS NECK. I MANAGED TO JUMP OFF IN TIME AND ROLLED DOWN HERE. BUT I THINK I BROKE MY ANKLE...
THIS IS THE END OF THE ROAD FOR ME, THORGAL. GO—I'LL COVER YOUR RETREAT. AT LEAST THAT'LL BE ONE GOOD THING I DO BEFORE I DIE.
IT'S WRONG TO ABAN-DON A WOUNDED ANIMAL, KRISS...
EVEN IF THAT ANIMAL IS A SNAKE. HOLD ON TO ME.
YOU DO KNOW HOW TO TALK TO A WOMAN.
THERE! LOOK!
THESE AREN'T HIS ARROWS. HE HAD SOMEONE WAITING FOR HIM.
PROBABLY THAT WOMAN HE TOLD US ABOUT. THEY CAN'T HAVE GONE FAR.
SPREAD OUT AND DRIVE THEM TOWARDS THE RAVINE! I'LL GIVE THE WOMAN TO THE FIRST MAN WHO SPOTS THEM.
21

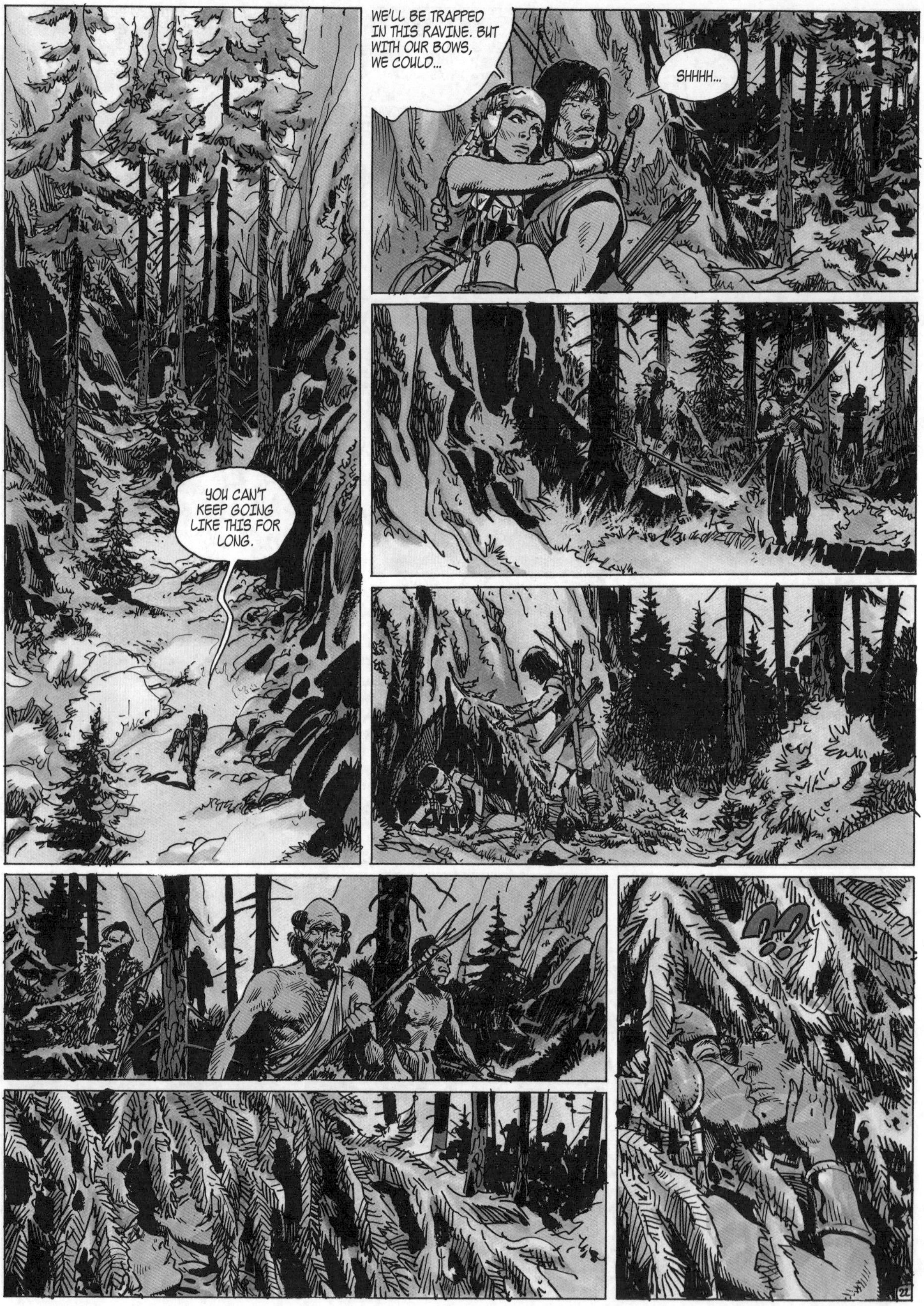
YOU CAN'T KEEP GOING LIKE THIS FOR LONG.
WE'LL BE TRAPPED IN THIS RAVINE. BUT WITH OUR BOWS, WE COULD...
SHHHH...
?!
22

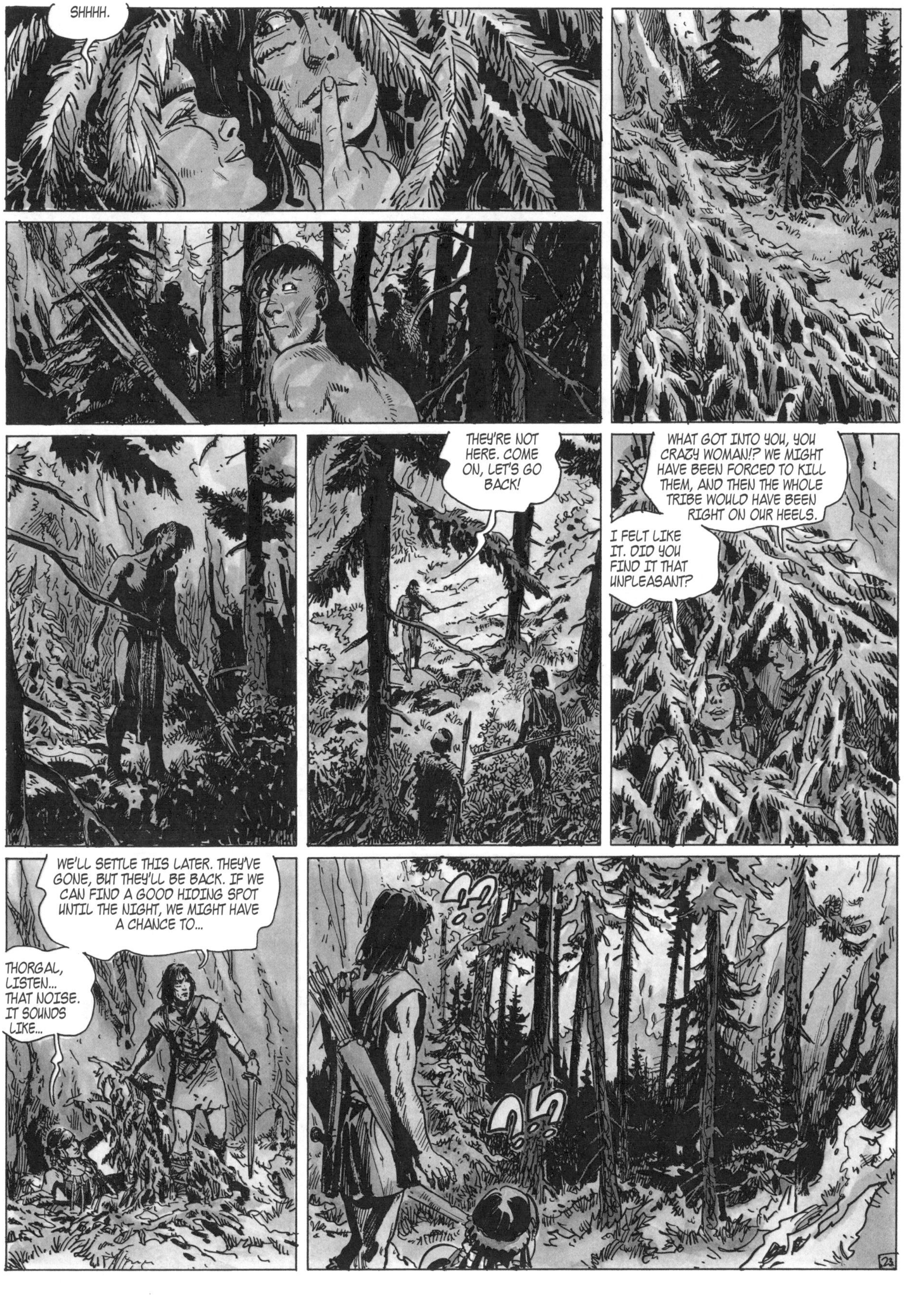
SHHHH.
THEY'RE NOT HERE. COME ON, LET'S GO BACK!
WHAT GOT INTO YOU, YOU CRAZY WOMAN!? WE MIGHT HAVE BEEN FORCED TO KILL THEM, AND THEN THE WHOLE TRIBE WOULD HAVE BEEN RIGHT ON OUR HEELS.
I FELT LIKE IT. DID YOU FIND IT THAT UNPLEASANT?
WE'LL SETTLE THIS LATER. THEY'VE GONE, BUT THEY'LL BE BACK. IF WE CAN FIND A GOOD HIDING SPOT UNTIL THE NIGHT, WE MIGHT HAVE A CHANCE TO...
THORGAL, LISTEN... THAT NOISE. IT SOUNDS LIKE...
23

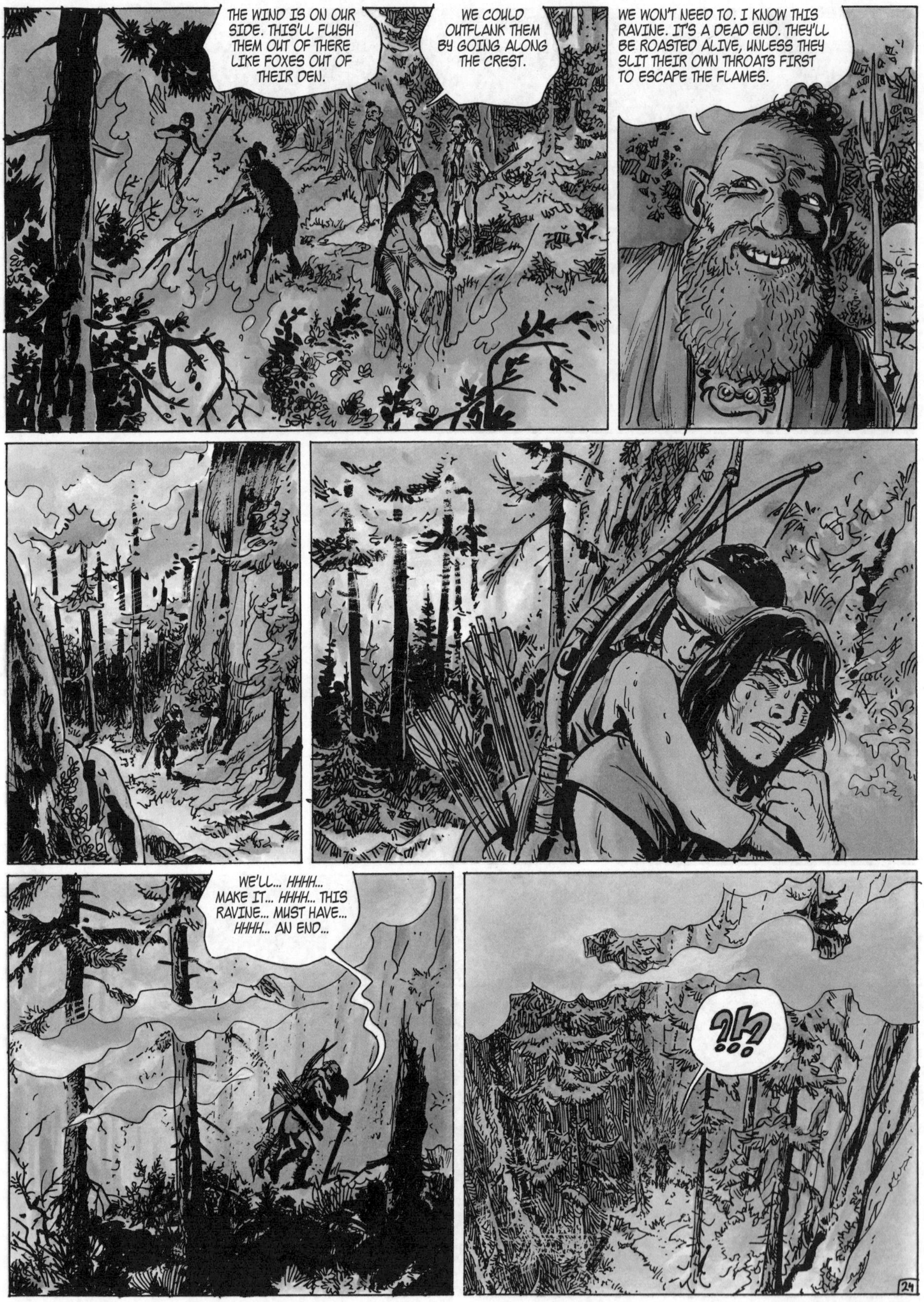
THE WIND IS ON OUR SIDE. THIS'LL FLUSH THEM OUT OF THERE LIKE FOXES OUT OF THEIR DEN.
WE COULD OUTFLANK THEM BY GOING ALONG THE CREST.
WE WON'T NEED TO. I KNOW THIS RAVINE. IT'S A DEAD END. THEY'LL BE ROASTED ALIVE, UNLESS THEY SLIT THEIR OWN THROATS FIRST TO ESCAPE THE FLAMES.
WE'LL... HHHH... MAKE IT... HHHH... THIS RAVINE... MUST HAVE... HHHH... AN END...
?!?!

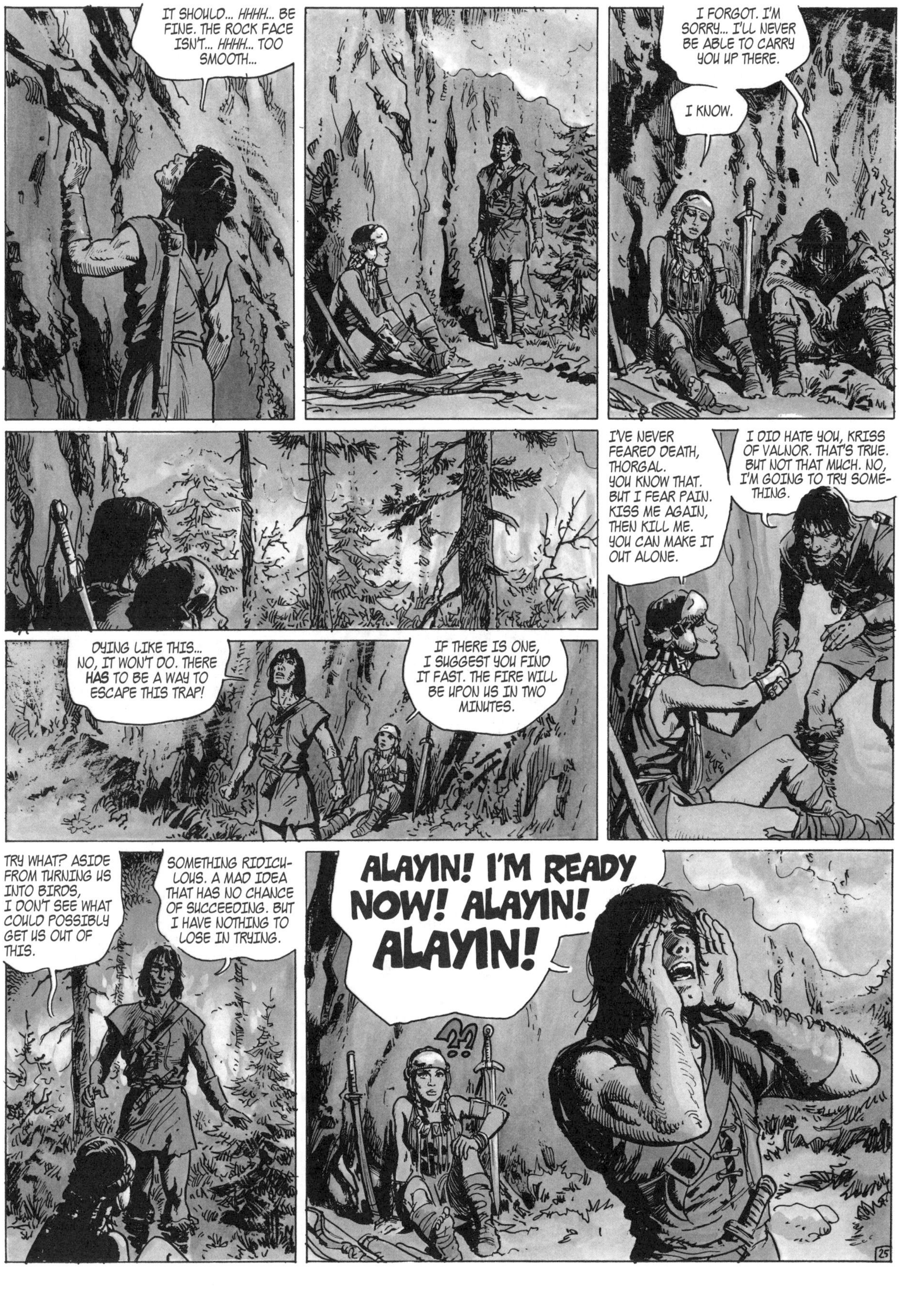

IT SHOULD... HHHH... BE FINE. THE ROCK FACE ISN'T... HHHH... TOO SMOOTH...
I FORGOT. I'M SORRY... I'LL NEVER BE ABLE TO CARRY YOU UP THERE.
I KNOW.
I'VE NEVER FEARED DEATH, THORGAL. YOU KNOW THAT. BUT I FEAR PAIN. KISS ME AGAIN, THEN KILL ME. YOU CAN MAKE IT OUT ALONE.
I DID HATE YOU, KRISS OF VALNOR. THAT'S TRUE. BUT NOT THAT MUCH. NO, I'M GOING TO TRY SOMETHING.
DYING LIKE THIS... NO, IT WON'T DO. THERE **HAS** TO BE A WAY TO ESCAPE THIS TRAP!
IF THERE IS ONE, I SUGGEST YOU FIND IT FAST. THE FIRE WILL BE UPON US IN TWO MINUTES.
TRY WHAT? ASIDE FROM TURNING US INTO BIRDS, I DON'T SEE WHAT COULD POSSIBLY GET US OUT OF THIS.
SOMETHING RIDICULOUS. A MAD IDEA THAT HAS NO CHANCE OF SUCCEEDING. BUT I HAVE NOTHING TO LOSE IN TRYING.
ALAYIN! I'M READY NOW! ALAYIN! ALAYIN!
?!?
25

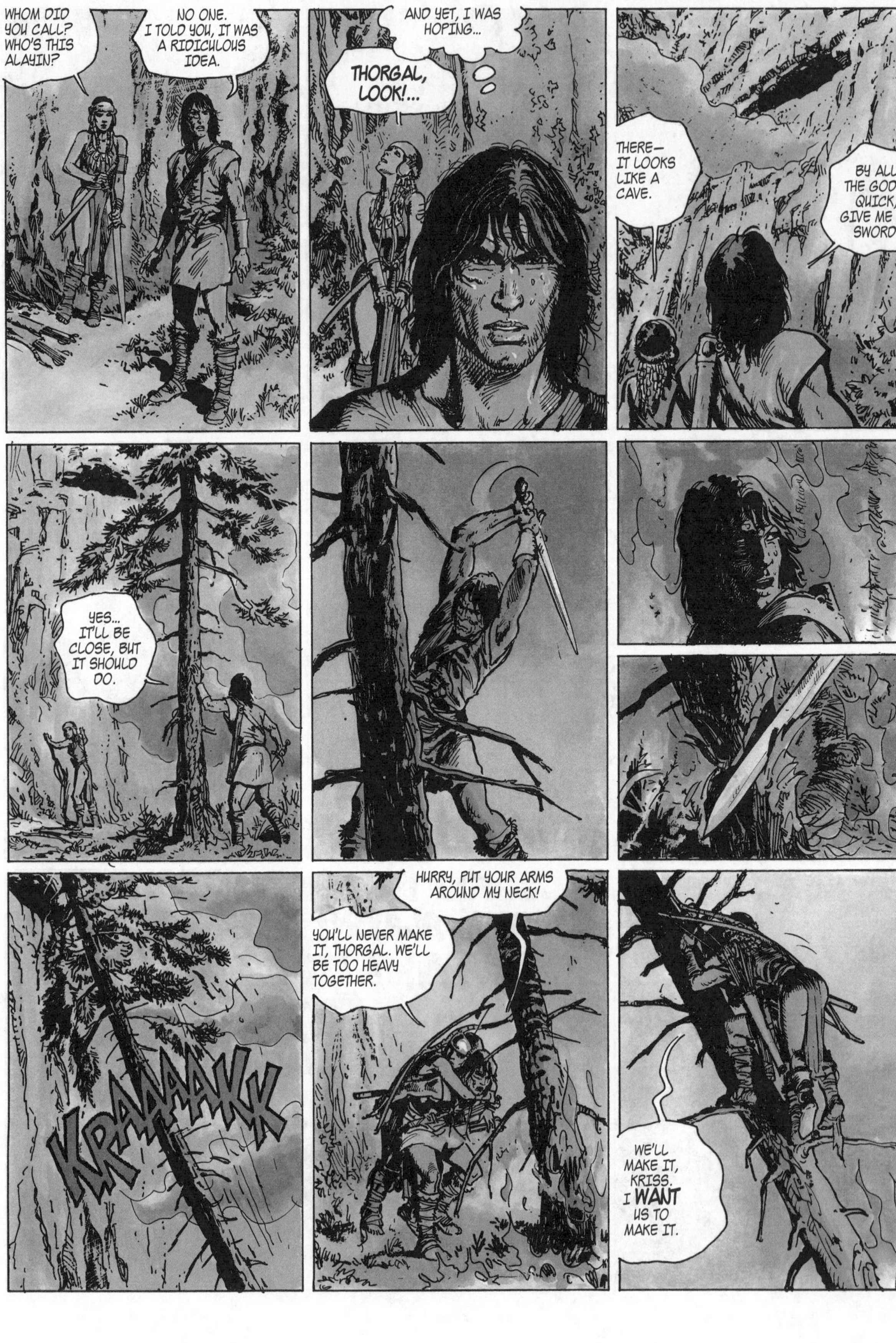
WHOM DID YOU CALL? WHO'S THIS ALAYIN?
NO ONE. I TOLD YOU, IT WAS A RIDICULOUS IDEA.
AND YET, I WAS HOPING...
THORGAL, LOOK!...
THERE— IT LOOKS LIKE A CAVE.
BY ALL THE GODS! QUICK, GIVE ME MY SWORD.
YES... IT'LL BE CLOSE, BUT IT SHOULD DO.
KRAAAAKK
HURRY, PUT YOUR ARMS AROUND MY NECK!
YOU'LL NEVER MAKE IT, THORGAL. WE'LL BE TOO HEAVY TOGETHER.
WE'LL MAKE IT, KRISS. I WANT US TO MAKE IT.
26

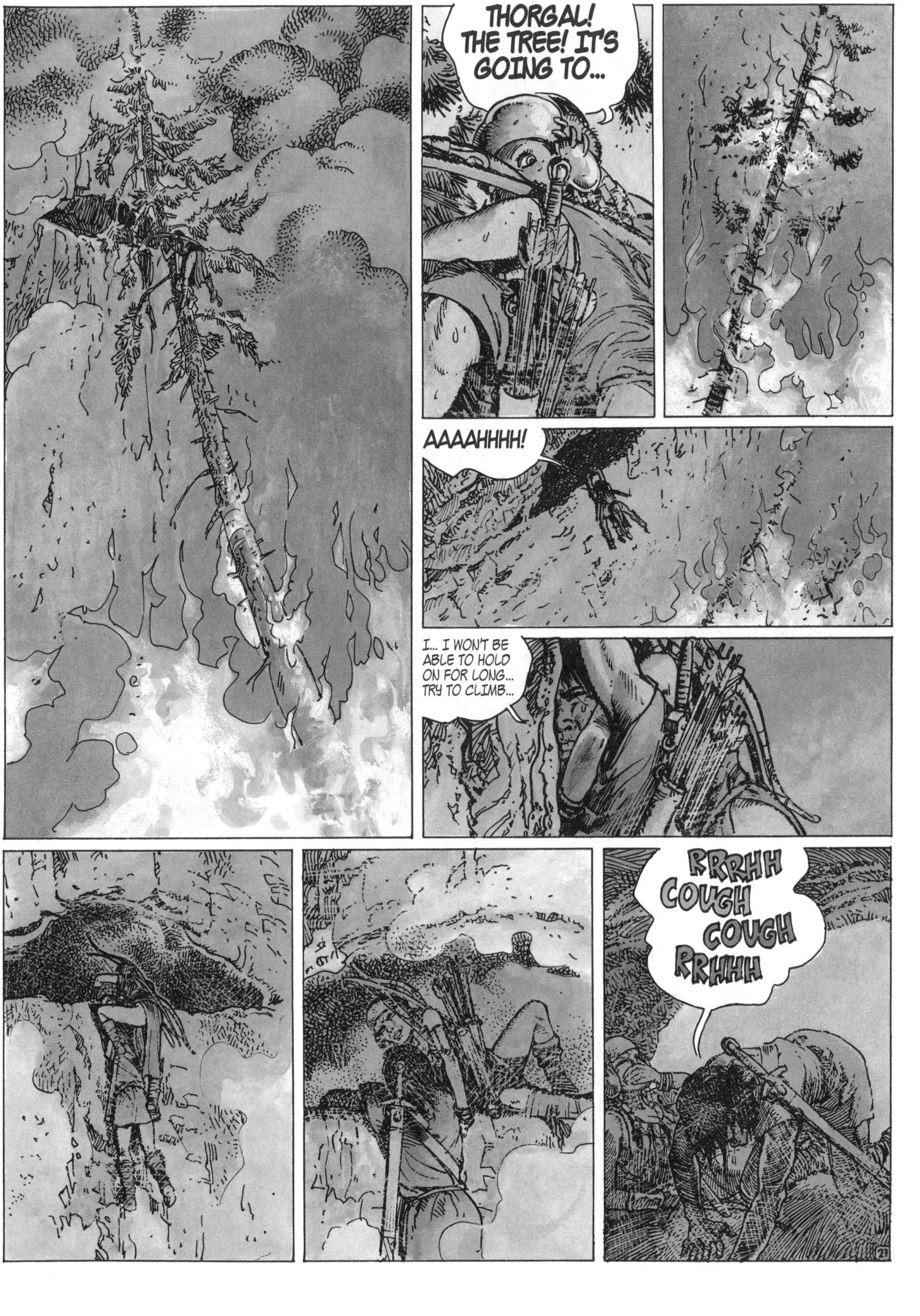
THORGAL! THE TREE! IT'S GOING TO...
AAAAHHHH!
I... I WON'T BE ABLE TO HOLD ON FOR LONG... TRY TO CLIMB...
RRRHH COUGH COUGH RRHHH

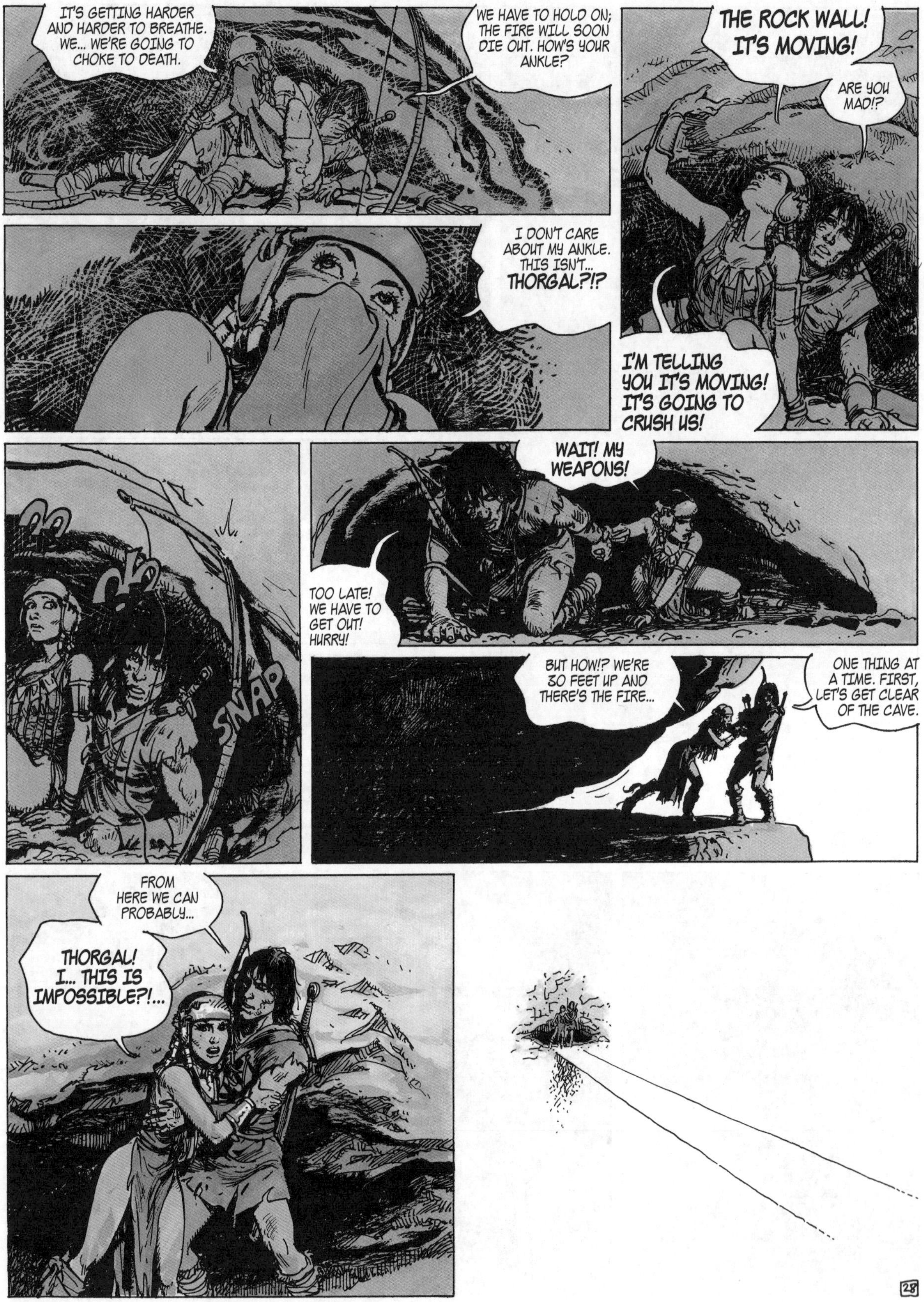

IT'S GETTING HARDER AND HARDER TO BREATHE. WE... WE'RE GOING TO CHOKE TO DEATH.
WE HAVE TO HOLD ON; THE FIRE WILL SOON DIE OUT. HOW'S YOUR ANKLE?
I DON'T CARE ABOUT MY ANKLE. THIS ISN'T... THORGAL?!?
THE ROCK WALL! IT'S MOVING!
ARE YOU MAD!?
I'M TELLING YOU IT'S MOVING! IT'S GOING TO CRUSH US!
SNAP
WAIT! MY WEAPONS!
TOO LATE! WE HAVE TO GET OUT! HURRY!
BUT HOW!? WE'RE 30 FEET UP AND THERE'S THE FIRE...
ONE THING AT A TIME. FIRST, LET'S GET CLEAR OF THE CAVE.
FROM HERE WE CAN PROBABLY...
THORGAL! I... THIS IS IMPOSSIBLE?!...
28

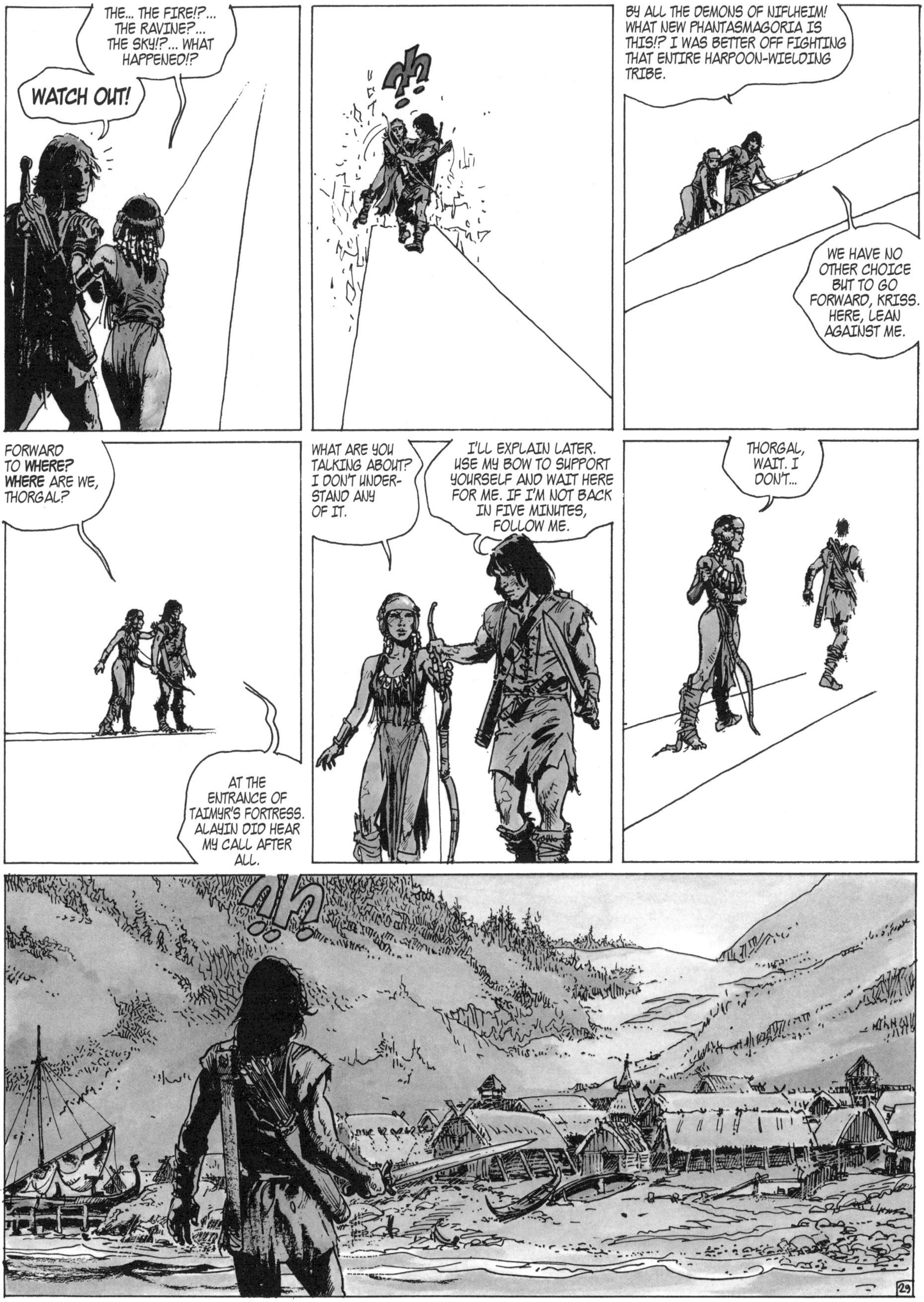
THE... THE FIRE!?... THE RAVINE?... THE SKY!?... WHAT HAPPENED!?
WATCH OUT!
BY ALL THE DEMONS OF NIFLHEIM! WHAT NEW PHANTASMAGORIA IS THIS!? I WAS BETTER OFF FIGHTING THAT ENTIRE HARPOON-WIELDING TRIBE.
WE HAVE NO OTHER CHOICE BUT TO GO FORWARD, KRISS. HERE, LEAN AGAINST ME.
FORWARD TO WHERE? WHERE ARE WE, THORGAL?
AT THE ENTRANCE OF TAIMYR'S FORTRESS. ALAYIN DID HEAR MY CALL AFTER ALL.
WHAT ARE YOU TALKING ABOUT? I DON'T UNDER-STAND ANY OF IT.
I'LL EXPLAIN LATER. USE MY BOW TO SUPPORT YOURSELF AND WAIT HERE FOR ME. IF I'M NOT BACK IN FIVE MINUTES, FOLLOW ME.
THORGAL, WAIT. I DON'T...
29

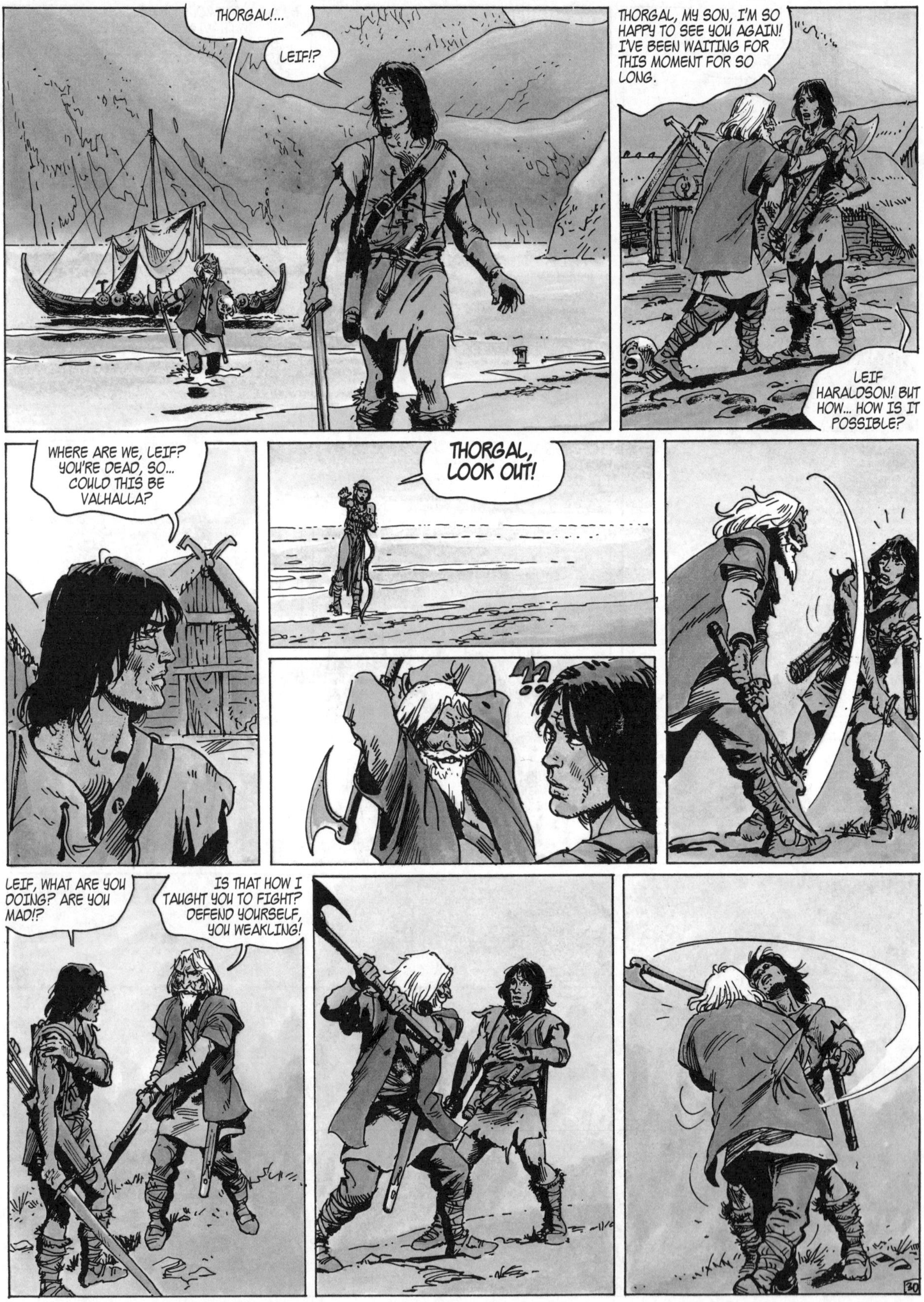

THORGAL!...
LEIF!?
THORGAL, MY SON, I'M SO HAPPY TO SEE YOU AGAIN! I'VE BEEN WAITING FOR THIS MOMENT FOR SO LONG.
LEIF HARALDSON! BUT HOW... HOW IS IT POSSIBLE?
WHERE ARE WE, LEIF? YOU'RE DEAD, SO... COULD THIS BE VALHALLA?
THORGAL, LOOK OUT!
?!
LEIF, WHAT ARE YOU DOING? ARE YOU MAD!?
IS THAT HOW I TAUGHT YOU TO FIGHT? DEFEND YOURSELF, YOU WEAKLING!
30

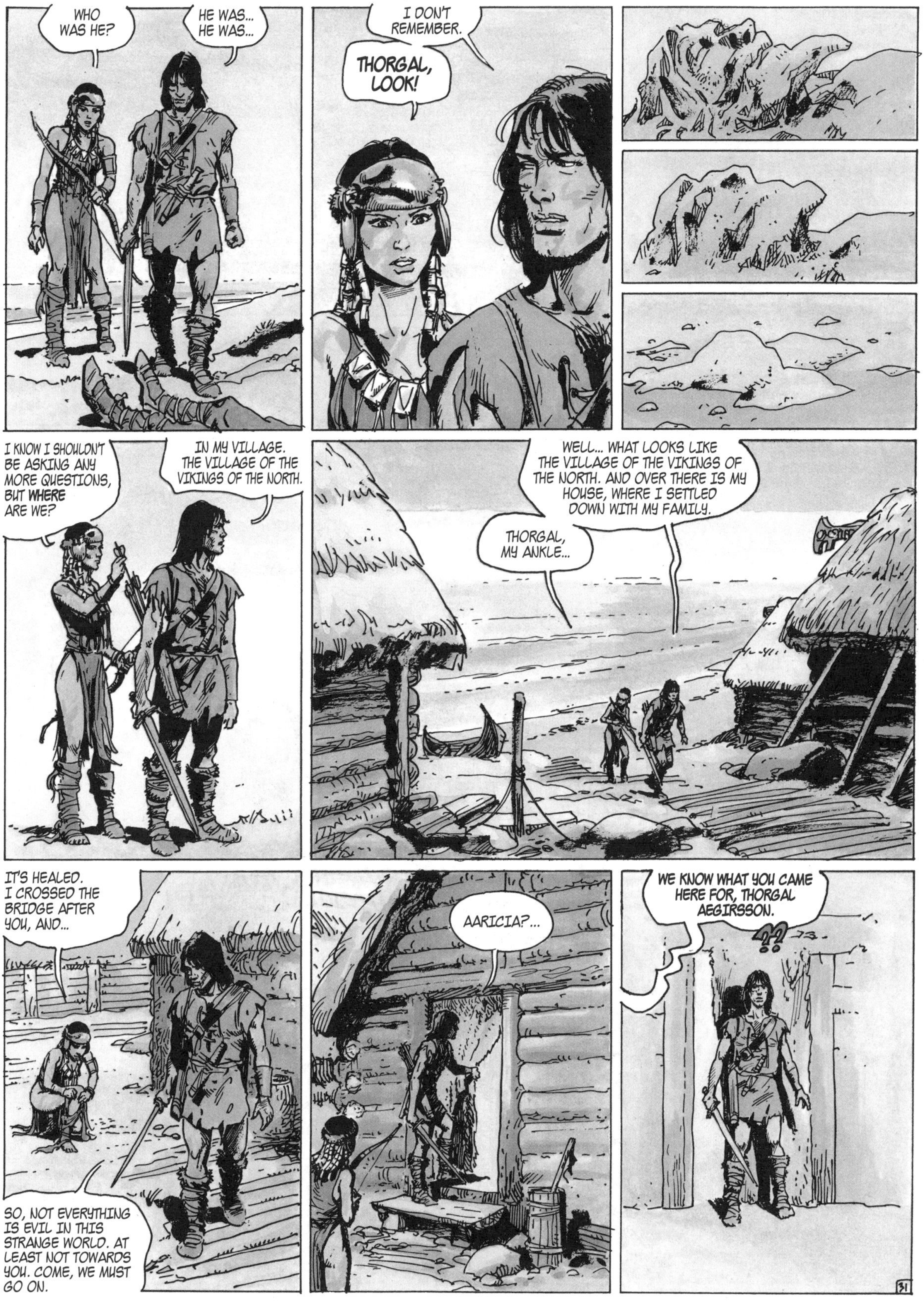
WHO WAS HE?
HE WAS... HE WAS...
I DON'T REMEMBER.
THORGAL, LOOK!
I KNOW I SHOULDN'T BE ASKING ANY MORE QUESTIONS, BUT WHERE ARE WE?
IN MY VILLAGE. THE VILLAGE OF THE VIKINGS OF THE NORTH.
WELL... WHAT LOOKS LIKE THE VILLAGE OF THE VIKINGS OF THE NORTH. AND OVER THERE IS MY HOUSE, WHERE I SETTLED DOWN WITH MY FAMILY.
THORGAL, MY ANKLE...
IT'S HEALED. I CROSSED THE BRIDGE AFTER YOU, AND...
SO, NOT EVERYTHING IS EVIL IN THIS STRANGE WORLD. AT LEAST NOT TOWARDS YOU. COME, WE MUST GO ON.
AARICIA?...
WE KNOW WHAT YOU CAME HERE FOR, THORGAL AEGIRSSON.
??
31

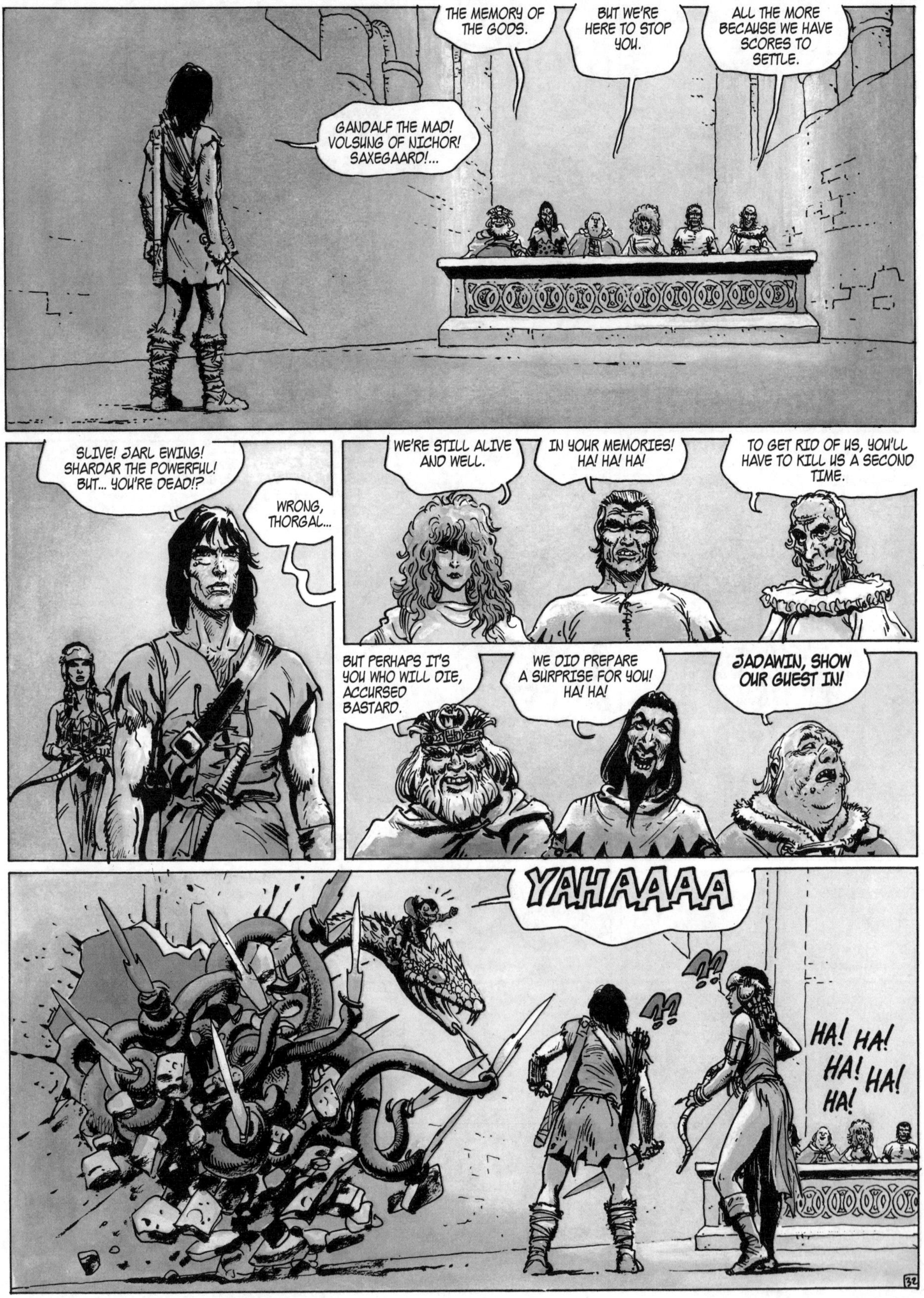
THE MEMORY OF THE GODS.
BUT WE'RE HERE TO STOP YOU.
ALL THE MORE BECAUSE WE HAVE SCORES TO SETTLE.
GANDALF THE MAD! VOLSUNG OF NICHOR! SAXEGAARD!...
SLIVE! JARL EWING! SHARDAR THE POWERFUL! BUT... YOU'RE DEAD!?
WRONG, THORGAL...
WE'RE STILL ALIVE AND WELL.
IN YOUR MEMORIES! HA! HA! HA!
TO GET RID OF US, YOU'LL HAVE TO KILL US A SECOND TIME.
BUT PERHAPS IT'S YOU WHO WILL DIE, ACCURSED BASTARD.
WE DID PREPARE A SURPRISE FOR YOU! HA! HA!
JADAWIN, SHOW OUR GUEST IN!
YAHAAAA
?!
?!
HA! HA! HA! HA! HA!
32

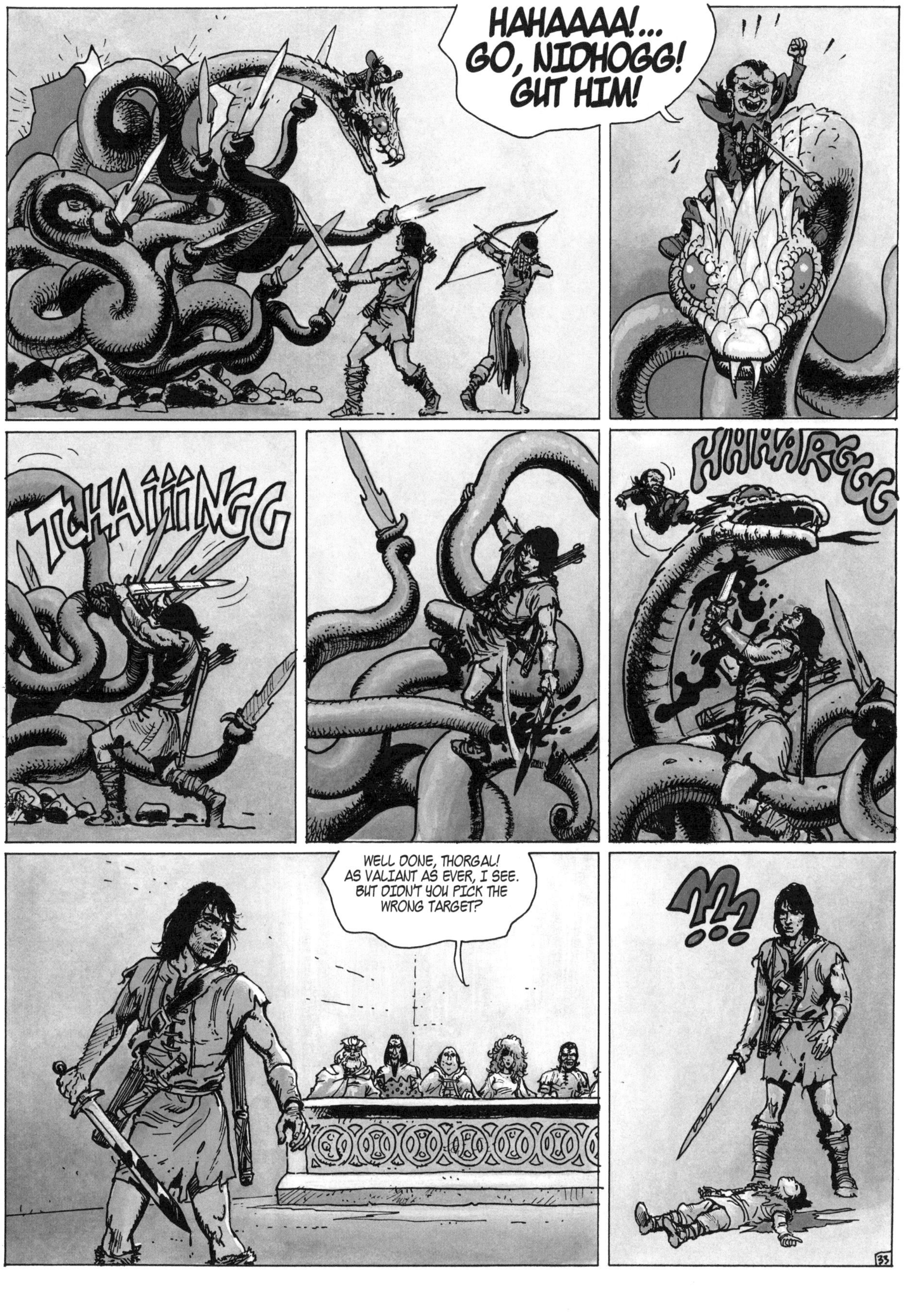
HAHAAAA!... GO, NIDHOGG! GUT HIM!
TCHAIIINGG
HHHARGGG
WELL DONE, THORGAL! AS VALIANT AS EVER, I SEE. BUT DIDN'T YOU PICK THE WRONG TARGET?
???
33

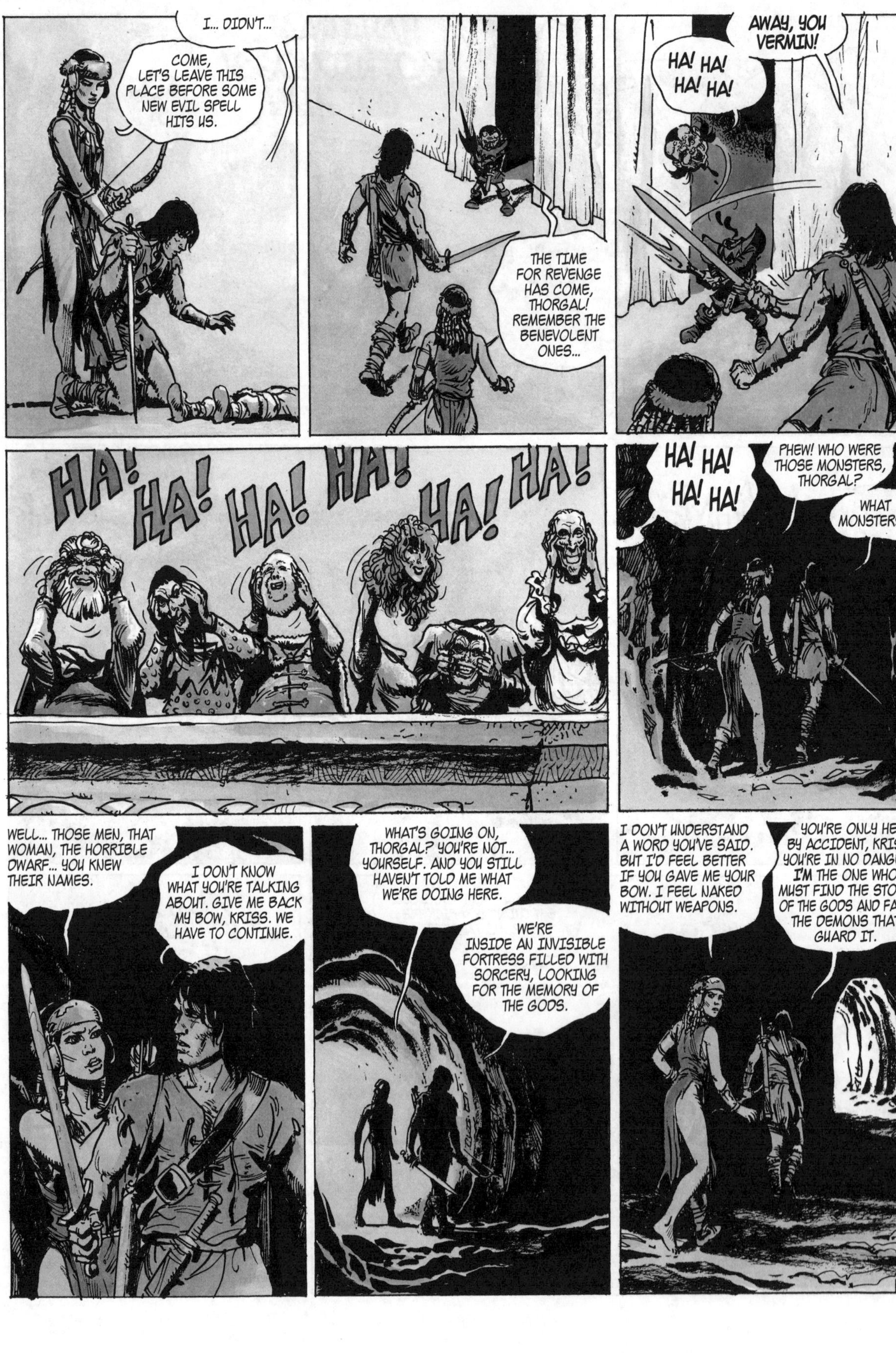

I... DIDN'T...
COME, LET'S LEAVE THIS PLACE BEFORE SOME NEW EVIL SPELL HITS US.
THE TIME FOR REVENGE HAS COME, THORGAL! REMEMBER THE BENEVOLENT ONES...
HA! HA! HA! HA!
AWAY, YOU VERMIN!
HA! HA! HA! HA! HA! HA!
HA! HA! HA! HA!
PHEW! WHO WERE THOSE MONSTERS, THORGAL?
WHAT MONSTERS?
WELL... THOSE MEN, THAT WOMAN, THE HORRIBLE DWARF... YOU KNEW THEIR NAMES.
I DON'T KNOW WHAT YOU'RE TALKING ABOUT. GIVE ME BACK MY BOW, KRISS. WE HAVE TO CONTINUE.
WHAT'S GOING ON, THORGAL? YOU'RE NOT... YOURSELF. AND YOU STILL HAVEN'T TOLD ME WHAT WE'RE DOING HERE.
WE'RE INSIDE AN INVISIBLE FORTRESS FILLED WITH SORCERY, LOOKING FOR THE MEMORY OF THE GODS.
I DON'T UNDERSTAND A WORD YOU'VE SAID. BUT I'D FEEL BETTER IF YOU GAVE ME YOUR BOW. I FEEL NAKED WITHOUT WEAPONS.
YOU'RE ONLY HERE BY ACCIDENT, KRISS. YOU'RE IN NO DANGER. I'M THE ONE WHO MUST FIND THE STONE OF THE GODS AND FACE THE DEMONS THAT GUARD IT.
34

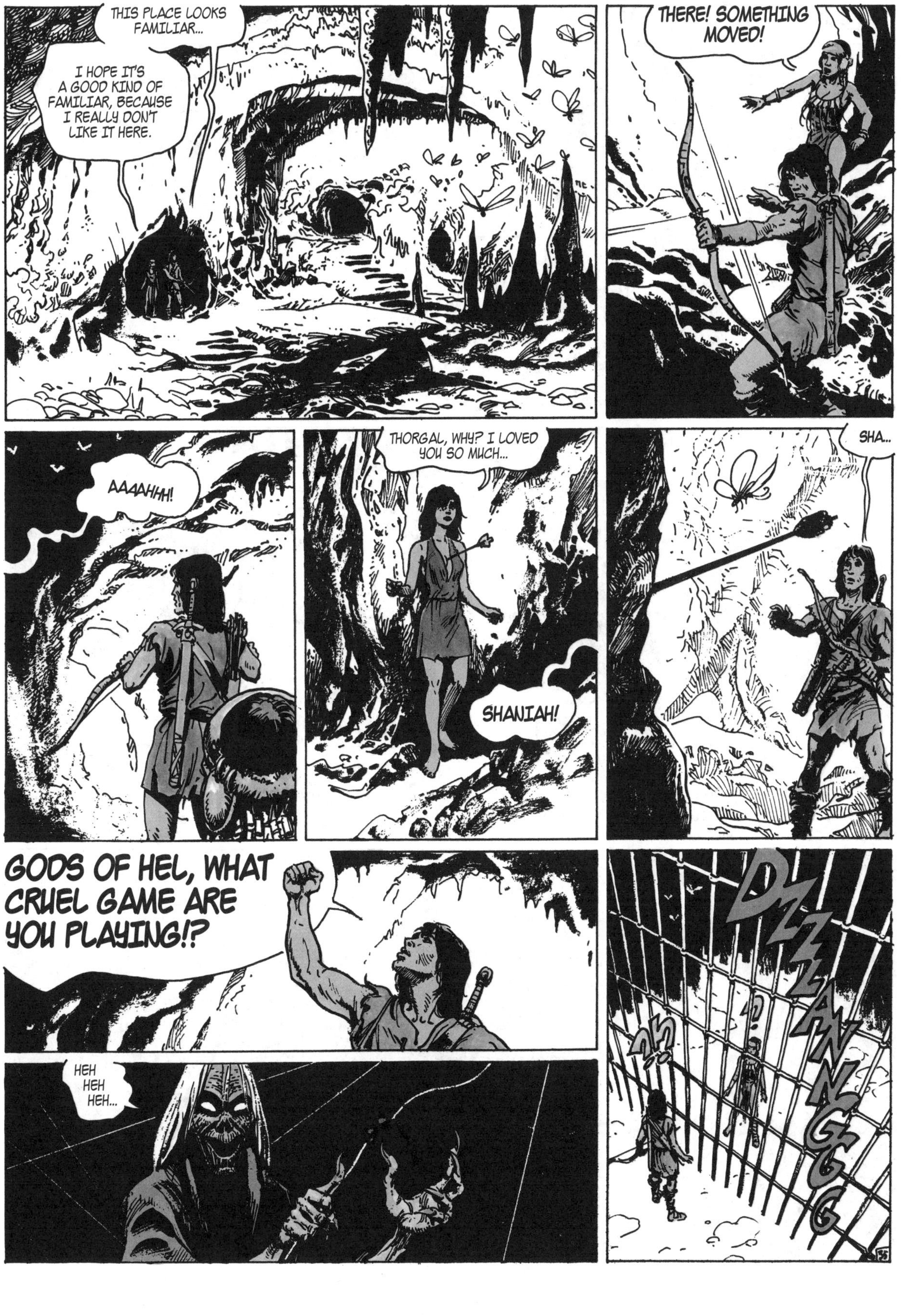
THIS PLACE LOOKS FAMILIAR...
I HOPE IT'S A GOOD KIND OF FAMILIAR, BECAUSE I REALLY DON'T LIKE IT HERE.
THERE! SOMETHING MOVED!
AAAAHHH!
THORGAL, WHY? I LOVED YOU SO MUCH...
SHANIAH!
SHA...
GODS OF HEL, WHAT CRUEL GAME ARE YOU PLAYING!?
HEH HEH HEH...
DZZZANNGGG

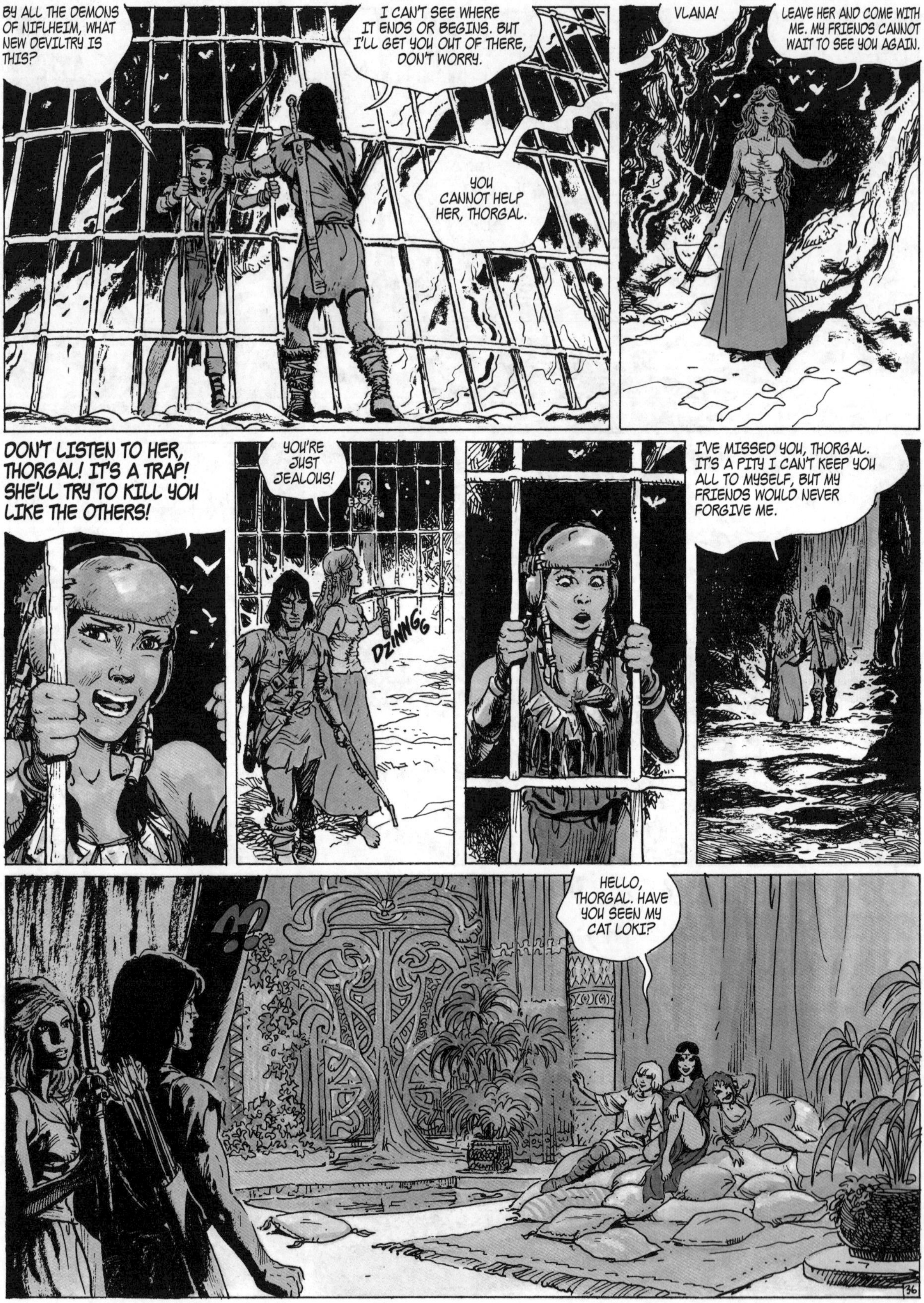
BY ALL THE DEMONS OF NIFLHEIM, WHAT NEW DEVILTRY IS THIS?
I CAN'T SEE WHERE IT ENDS OR BEGINS. BUT I'LL GET YOU OUT OF THERE, DON'T WORRY.
YOU CANNOT HELP HER, THORGAL.
VLANA!
LEAVE HER AND COME WITH ME. MY FRIENDS CANNOT WAIT TO SEE YOU AGAIN.
DON'T LISTEN TO HER, THORGAL! IT'S A TRAP! SHE'LL TRY TO KILL YOU LIKE THE OTHERS!
YOU'RE JUST JEALOUS!
DZINNGG
I'VE MISSED YOU, THORGAL. IT'S A PITY I CAN'T KEEP YOU ALL TO MYSELF, BUT MY FRIENDS WOULD NEVER FORGIVE ME.
HELLO, THORGAL. HAVE YOU SEEN MY CAT LOKI?
?!
36

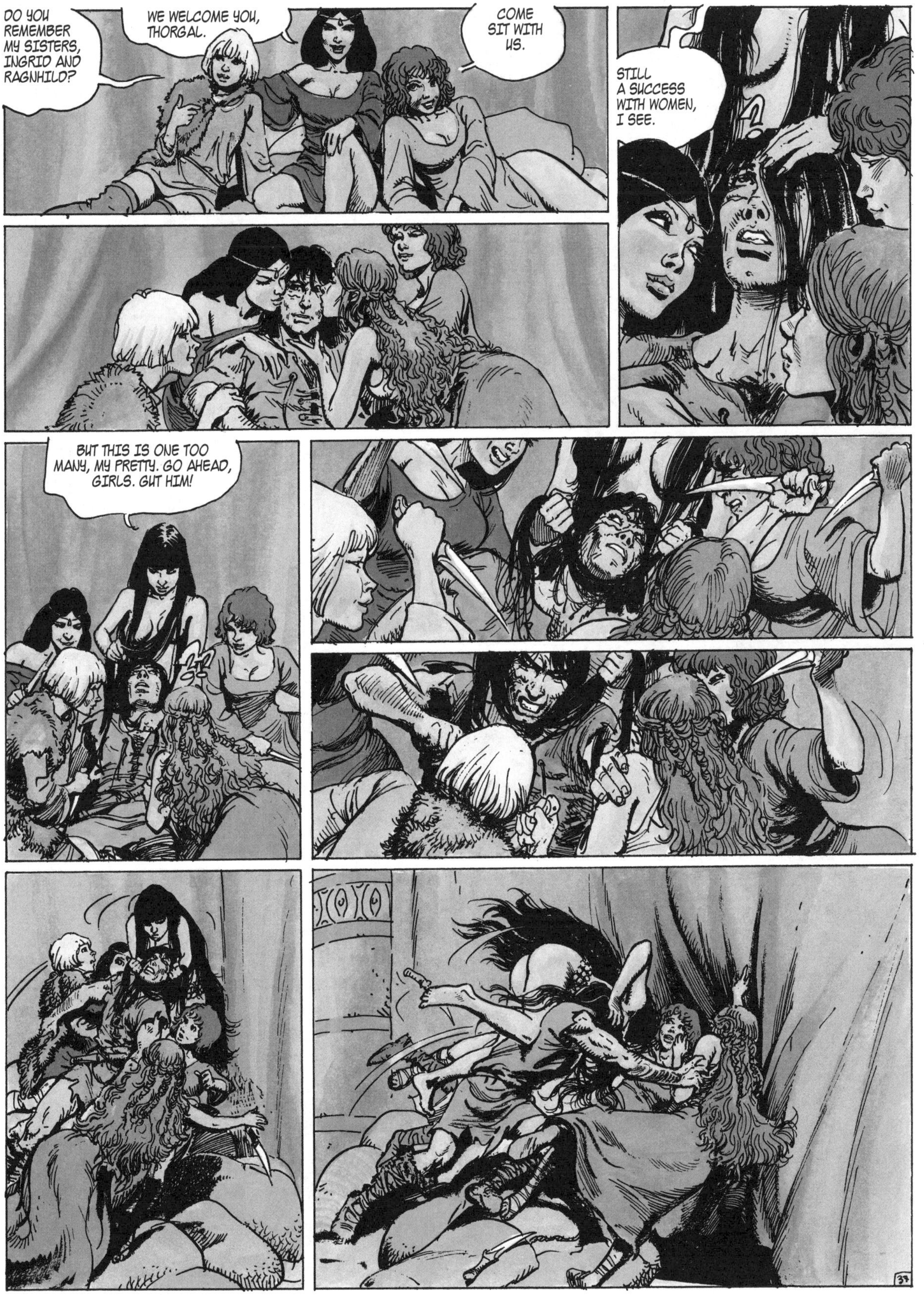
DO YOU REMEMBER MY SISTERS, INGRID AND RAGNHILD?
WE WELCOME YOU, THORGAL.
COME SIT WITH US.
STILL A SUCCESS WITH WOMEN, I SEE.
BUT THIS IS ONE TOO MANY, MY PRETTY. GO AHEAD, GIRLS. GUT HIM!

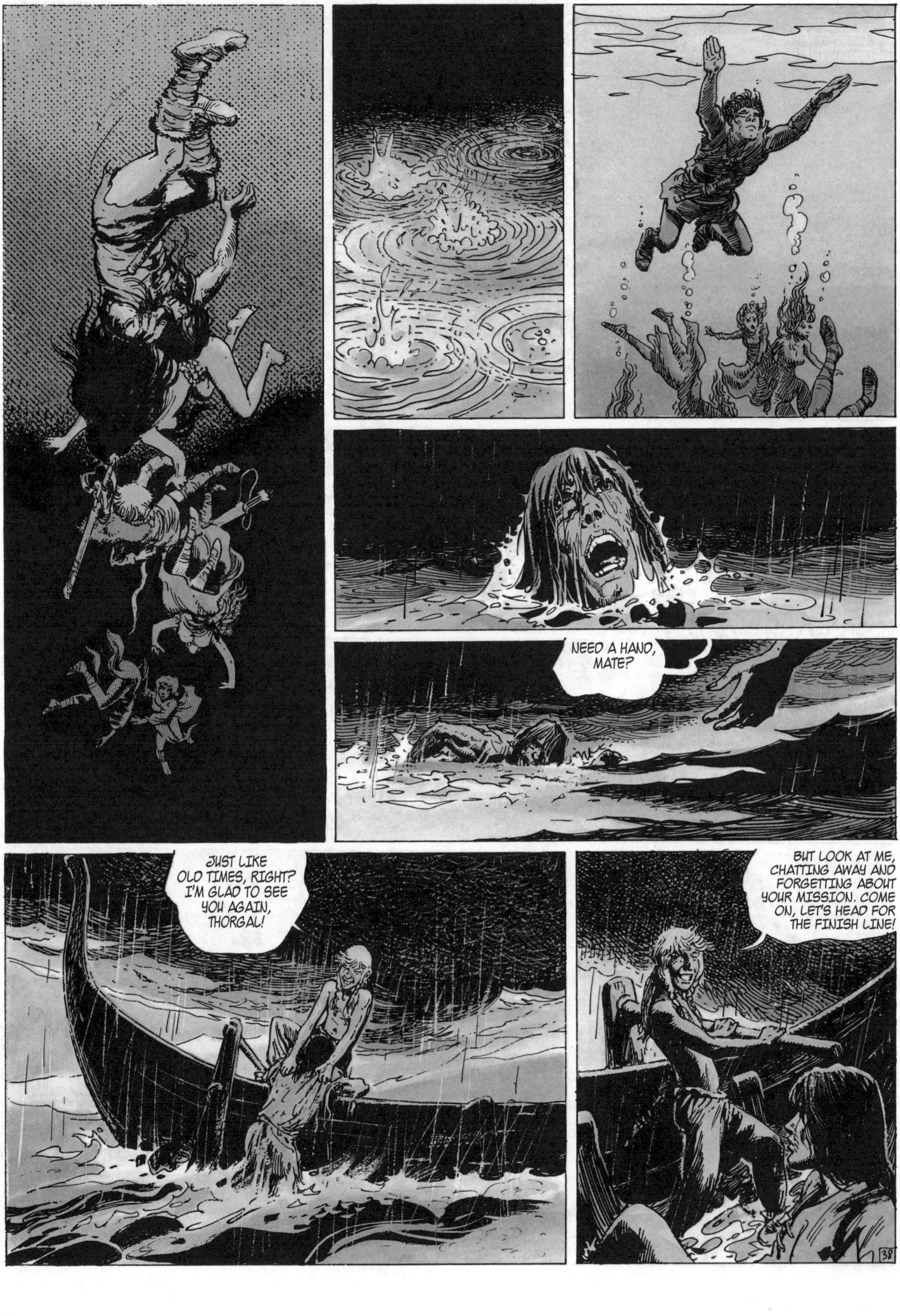
NEED A HAND, MATE?
JUST LIKE OLD TIMES, RIGHT? I'M GLAD TO SEE YOU AGAIN, THORGAL!
BUT LOOK AT ME, CHATTING AWAY AND FORGETTING ABOUT YOUR MISSION. COME ON, LET'S HEAD FOR THE FINISH LINE!
38

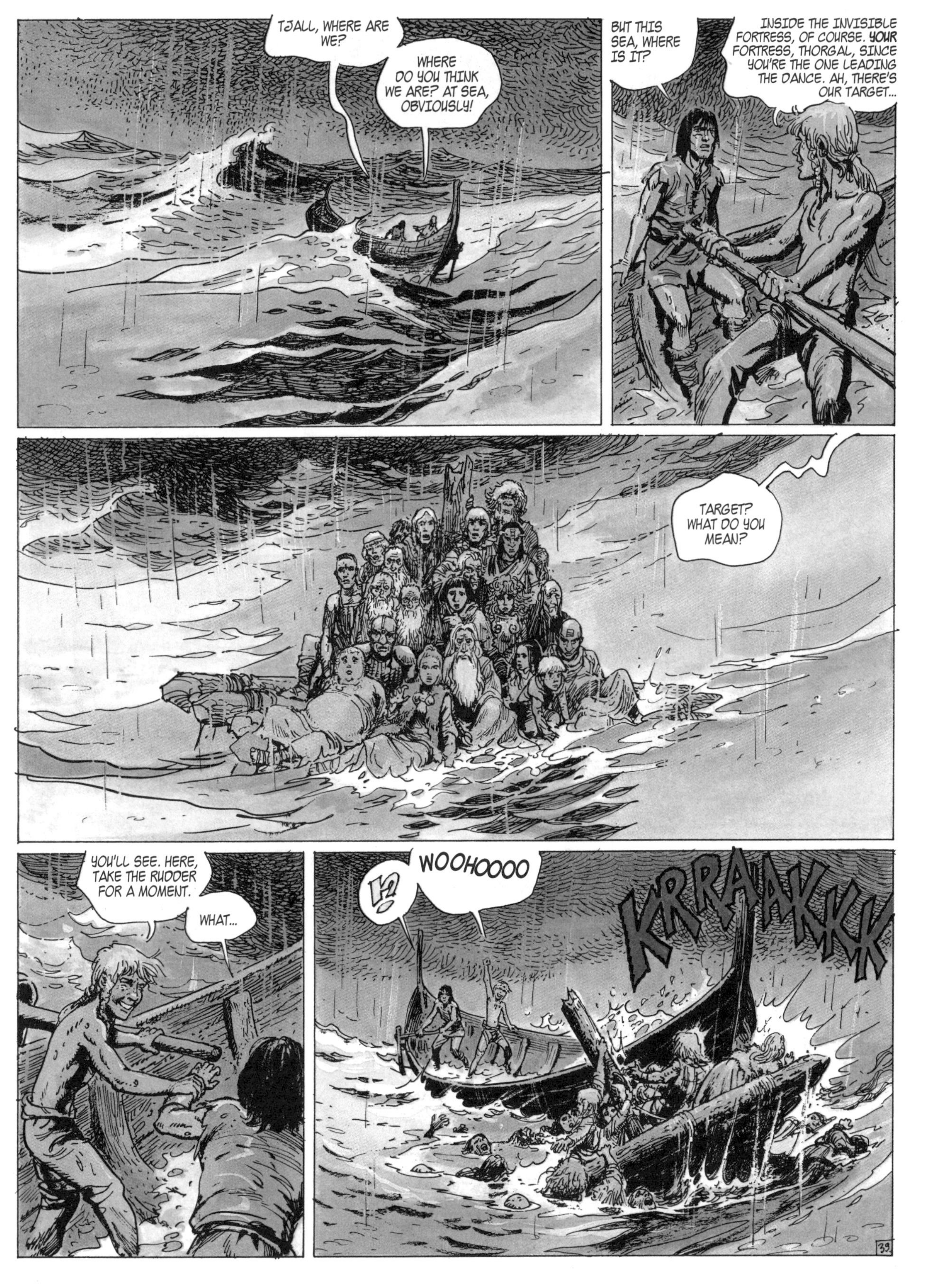
TJALL, WHERE ARE WE?
WHERE DO YOU THINK WE ARE? AT SEA, OBVIOUSLY!
BUT THIS SEA, WHERE IS IT?
INSIDE THE INVISIBLE FORTRESS, OF COURSE. YOUR FORTRESS, THORGAL, SINCE YOU'RE THE ONE LEADING THE DANCE. AH, THERE'S OUR TARGET...
TARGET? WHAT DO YOU MEAN?
YOU'LL SEE. HERE, TAKE THE RUDDER FOR A MOMENT.
WHAT...
!?
WOOHOOOO
KRRAAKKK
39

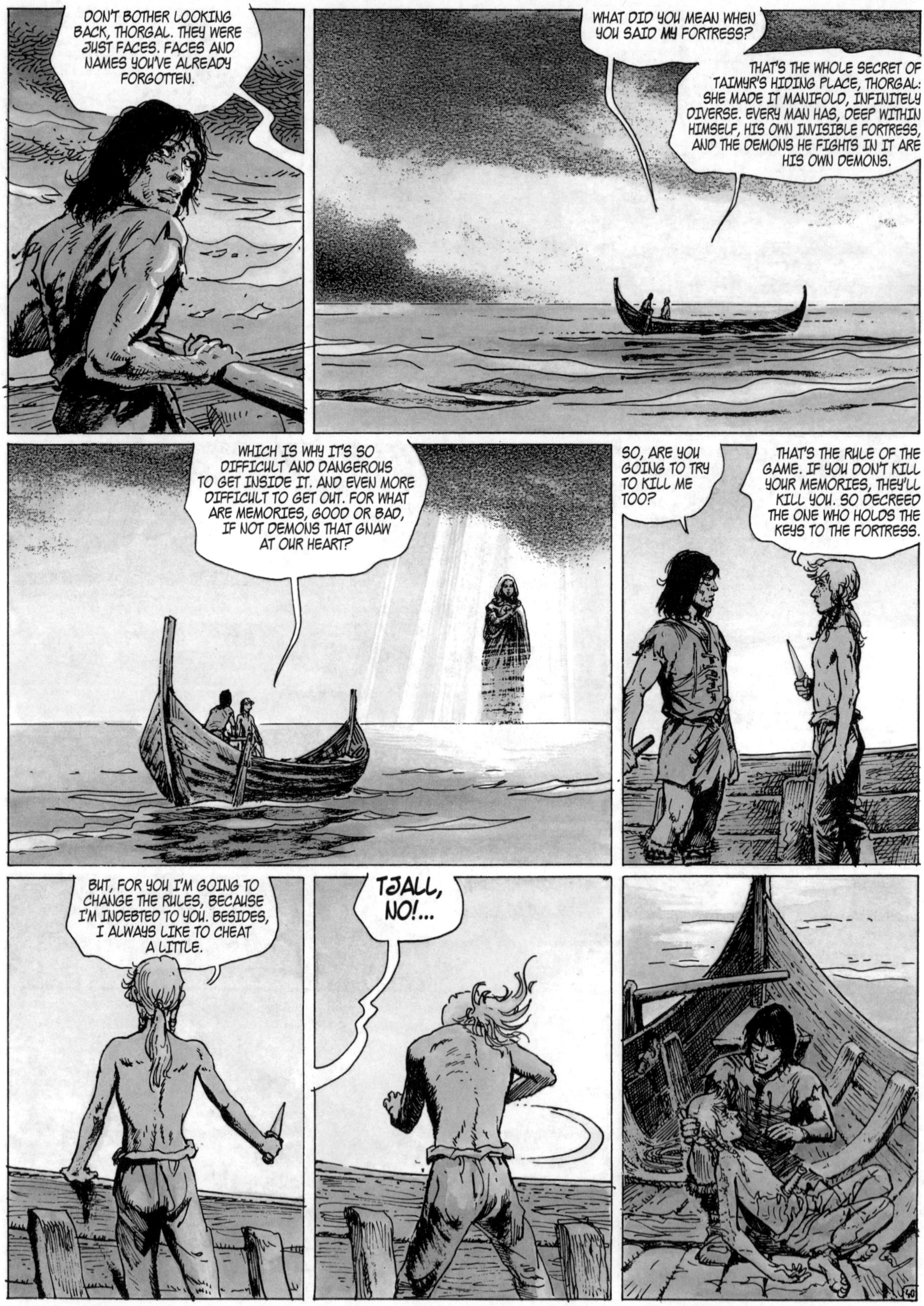
DON'T BOTHER LOOKING BACK, THORGAL. THEY WERE JUST FACES. FACES AND NAMES YOU'VE ALREADY FORGOTTEN.
WHAT DID YOU MEAN WHEN YOU SAID MY FORTRESS?
THAT'S THE WHOLE SECRET OF TAIMYR'S HIDING PLACE, THORGAL: SHE MADE IT MANIFOLD, INFINITELY DIVERSE. EVERY MAN HAS, DEEP WITHIN HIMSELF, HIS OWN INVISIBLE FORTRESS, AND THE DEMONS HE FIGHTS IN IT ARE HIS OWN DEMONS.
WHICH IS WHY IT'S SO DIFFICULT AND DANGEROUS TO GET INSIDE IT. AND EVEN MORE DIFFICULT TO GET OUT. FOR WHAT ARE MEMORIES, GOOD OR BAD, IF NOT DEMONS THAT GNAW AT OUR HEART?
SO, ARE YOU GOING TO TRY TO KILL ME TOO?
THAT'S THE RULE OF THE GAME. IF YOU DON'T KILL YOUR MEMORIES, THEY'LL KILL YOU. SO DECREED THE ONE WHO HOLDS THE KEYS TO THE FORTRESS.
BUT, FOR YOU I'M GOING TO CHANGE THE RULES, BECAUSE I'M INDEBTED TO YOU. BESIDES, I ALWAYS LIKE TO CHEAT A LITTLE.
TJALL, NO!...

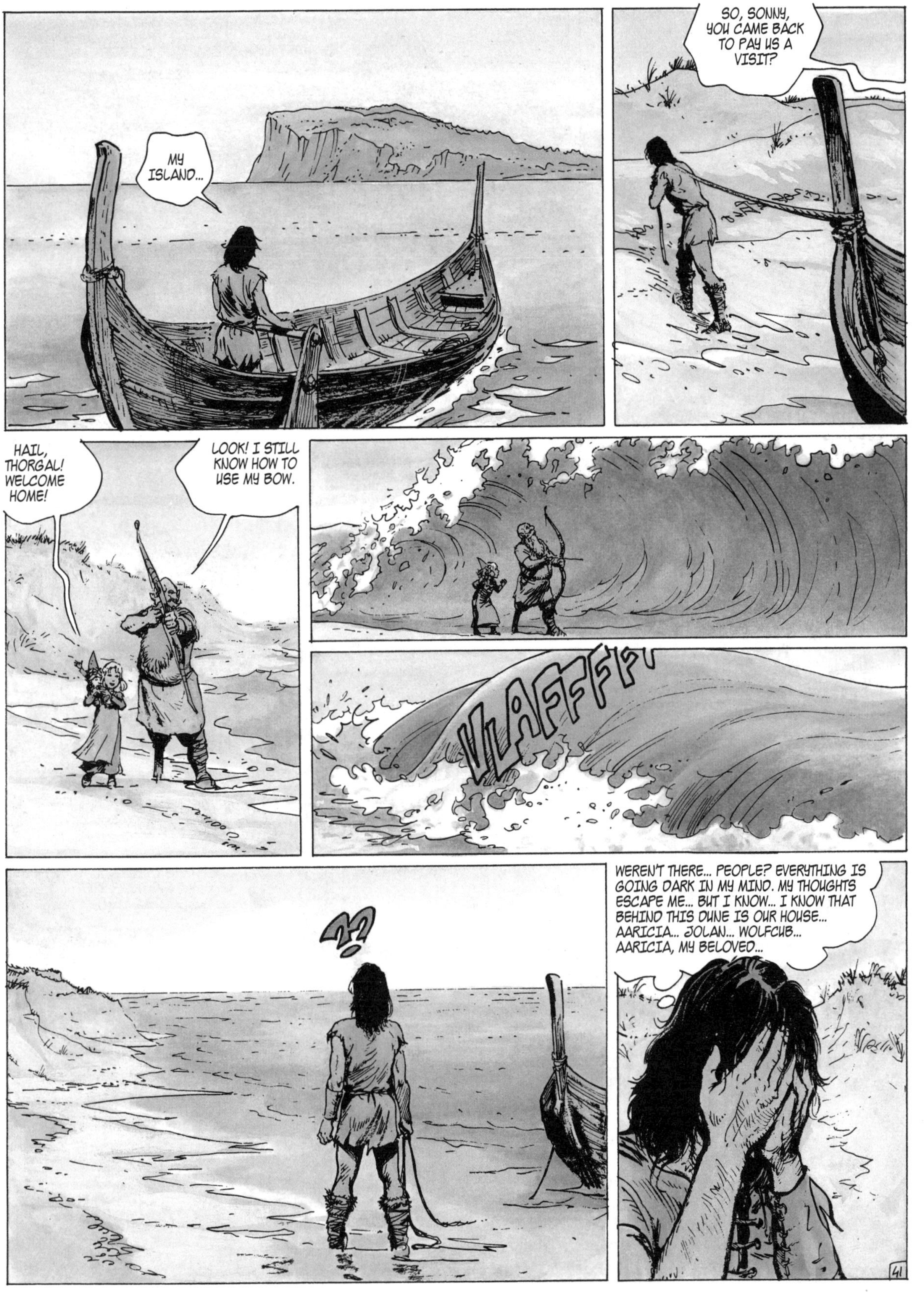
MY ISLAND...
SO, SONNY, YOU CAME BACK TO PAY US A VISIT?
HAIL, THORGAL! WELCOME HOME!
LOOK! I STILL KNOW HOW TO USE MY BOW.
VLAFFFF
WEREN'T THERE... PEOPLE? EVERYTHING IS GOING DARK IN MY MIND. MY THOUGHTS ESCAPE ME... BUT I KNOW... I KNOW THAT BEHIND THIS DUNE IS OUR HOUSE... AARICIA... JOLAN... WOLFCUB... AARICIA, MY BELOVED...
41

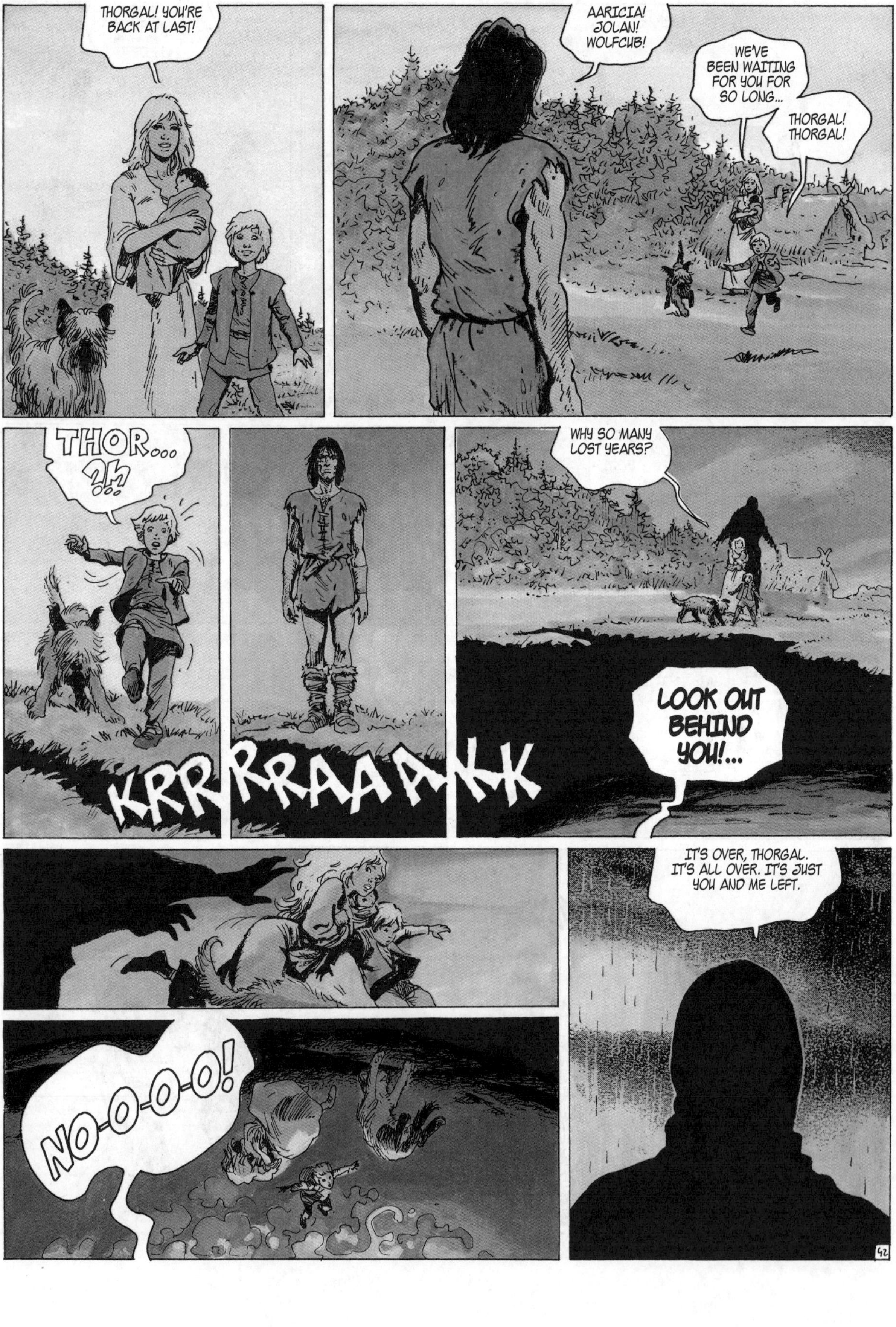
THORGAL! YOU'RE BACK AT LAST!
AARICIA! JOLAN! WOLFCUB!
WE'VE BEEN WAITING FOR YOU FOR SO LONG...
THORGAL! THORGAL!
THOR...
?!
WHY SO MANY LOST YEARS?
KRRRRAAAKK
LOOK OUT BEHIND YOU!...
IT'S OVER, THORGAL. IT'S ALL OVER. IT'S JUST YOU AND ME LEFT.
NO-O-O-O!
42

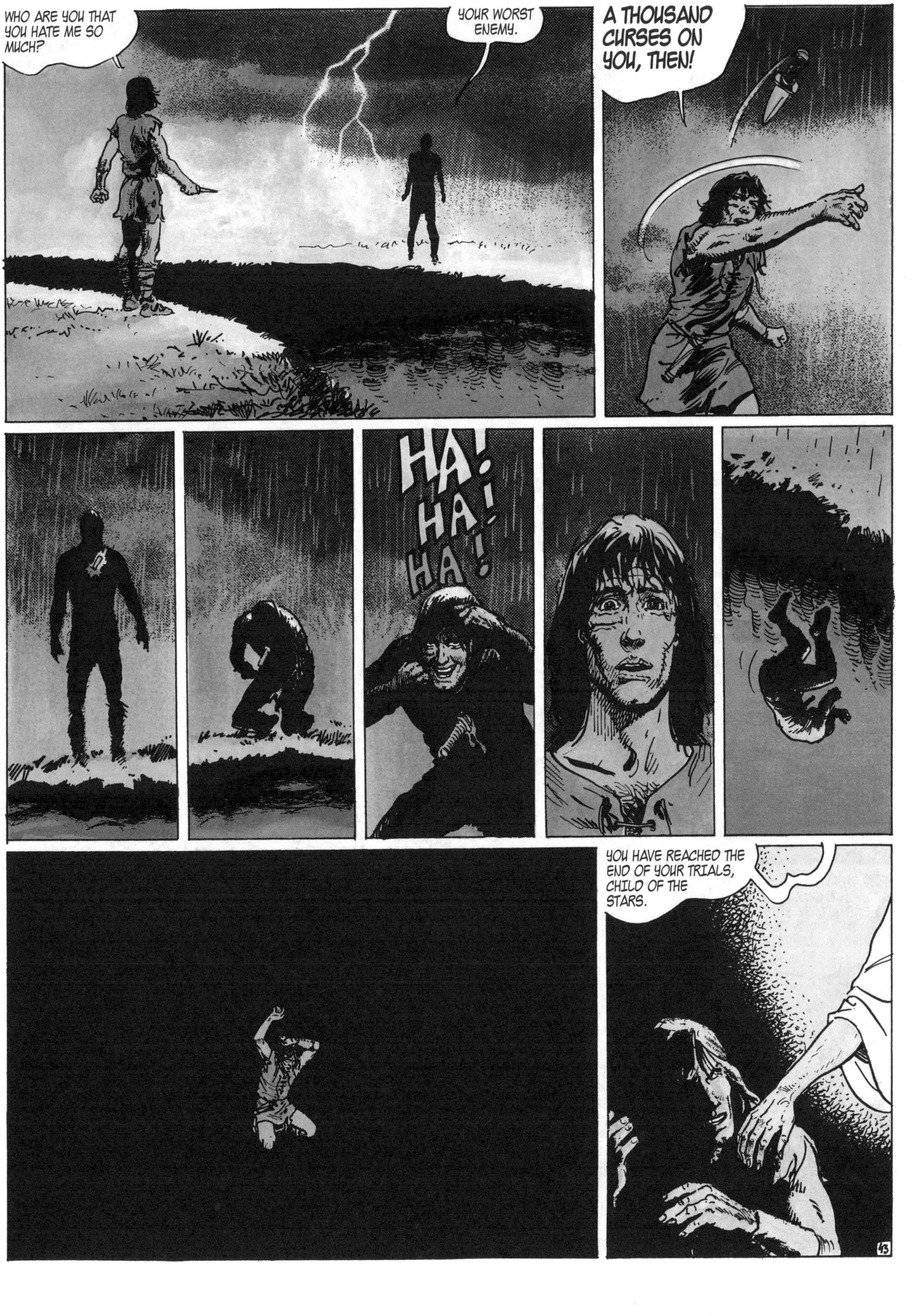
WHO ARE YOU THAT YOU HATE ME SO MUCH?
YOUR WORST ENEMY.
A THOUSAND CURSES ON YOU, THEN!
HA! HA! HA!
YOU HAVE REACHED THE END OF YOUR TRIALS, CHILD OF THE STARS.
43

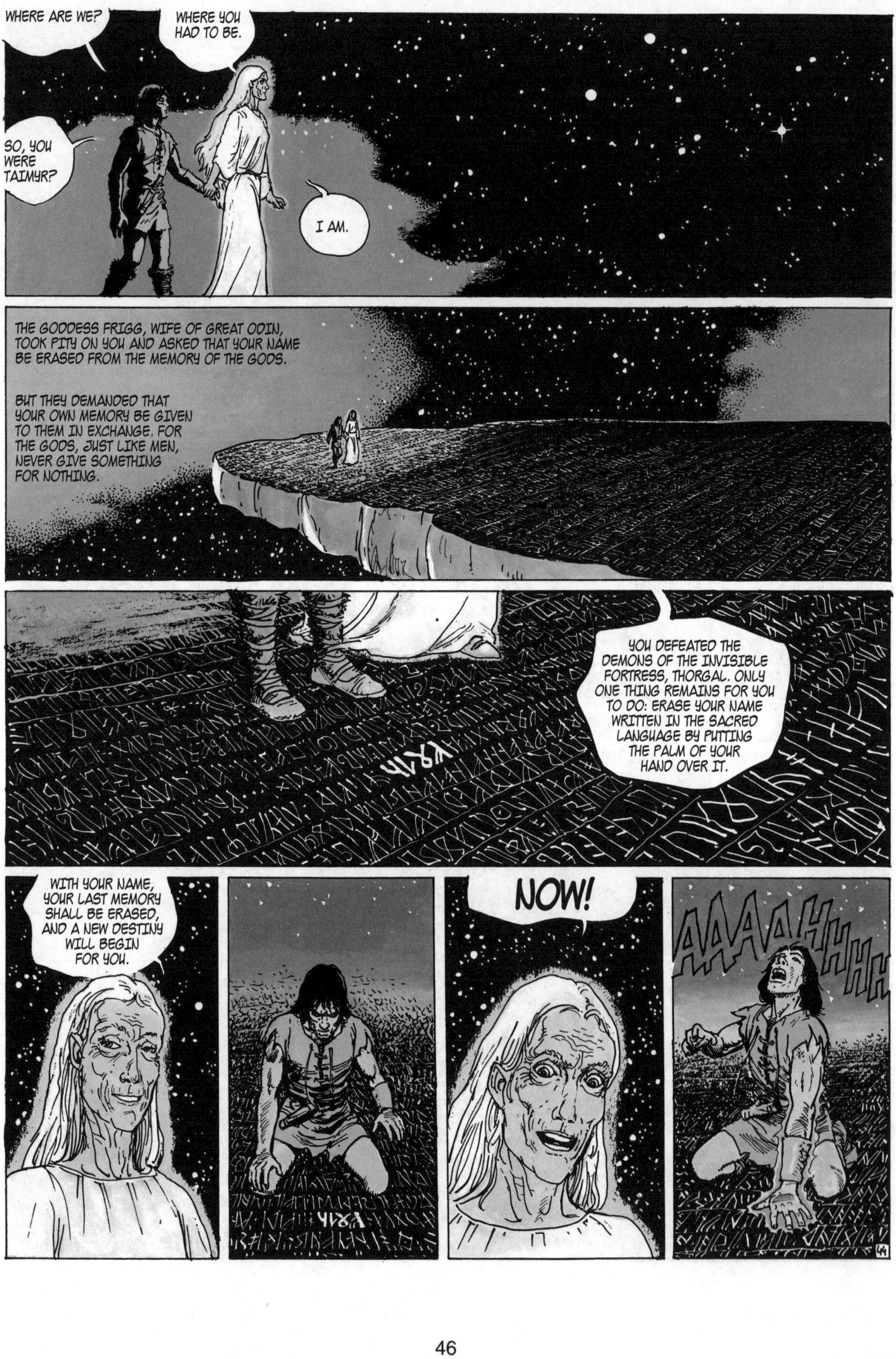
WHERE ARE WE?
WHERE YOU HAD TO BE.
SO, YOU WERE TAIMYR?
I AM.
THE GODDESS FRIGG, WIFE OF GREAT ODIN, TOOK PITY ON YOU AND ASKED THAT YOUR NAME BE ERASED FROM THE MEMORY OF THE GODS.
BUT THEY DEMANDED THAT YOUR OWN MEMORY BE GIVEN TO THEM IN EXCHANGE. FOR THE GODS, JUST LIKE MEN, NEVER GIVE SOMETHING FOR NOTHING.
YOU DEFEATED THE DEMONS OF THE INVISIBLE FORTRESS, THORGAL. ONLY ONE THING REMAINS FOR YOU TO DO: ERASE YOUR NAME WRITTEN IN THE SACRED LANGUAGE BY PUTTING THE PALM OF YOUR HAND OVER IT.
WITH YOUR NAME, YOUR LAST MEMORY SHALL BE ERASED, AND A NEW DESTINY WILL BEGIN FOR YOU.
NOW!
AAAAAHHHH
44

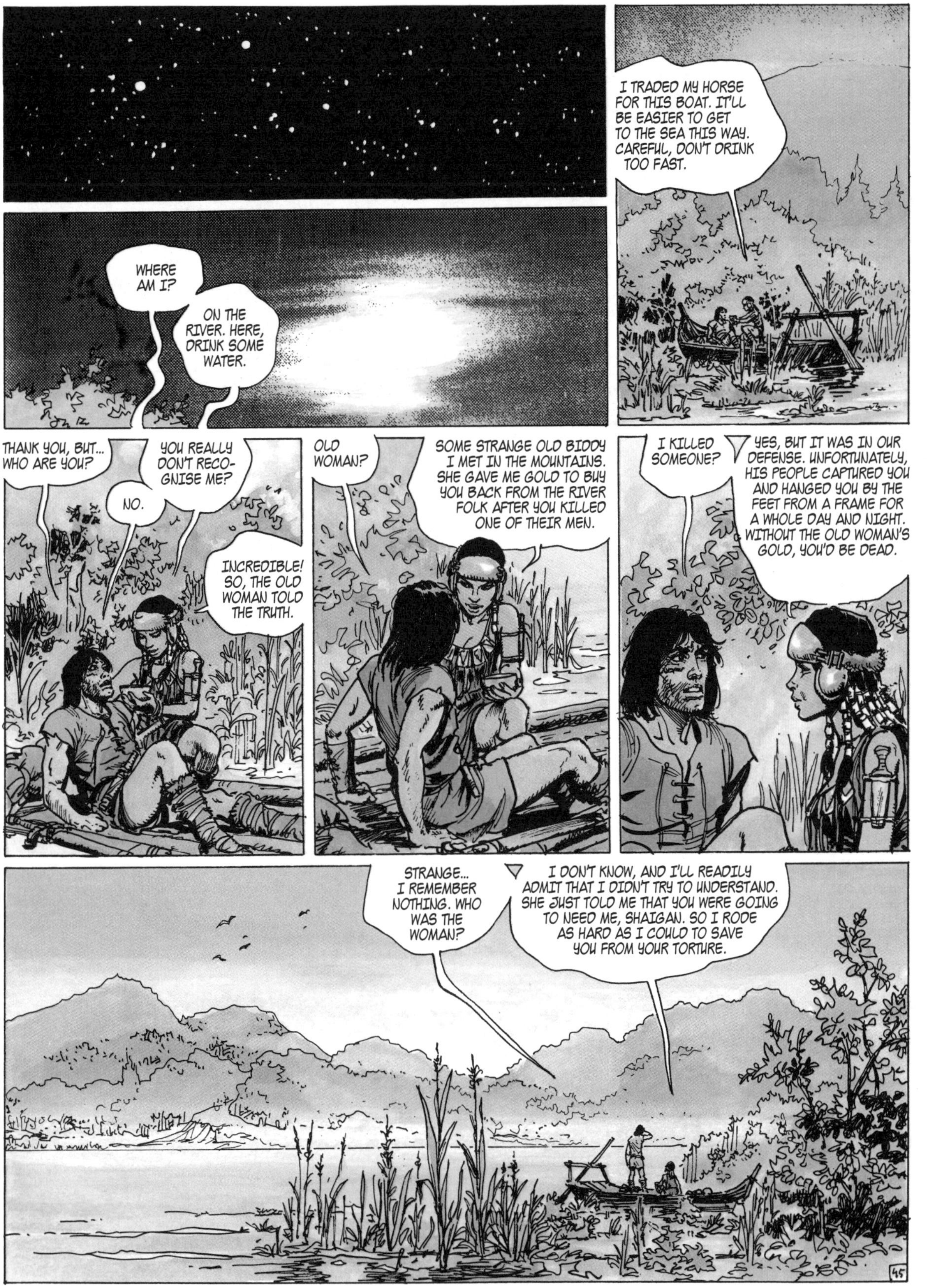
I TRADED MY HORSE FOR THIS BOAT. IT'LL BE EASIER TO GET TO THE SEA THIS WAY. CAREFUL, DON'T DRINK TOO FAST.
WHERE AM I?
ON THE RIVER. HERE, DRINK SOME WATER.
THANK YOU, BUT... WHO ARE YOU?
YOU REALLY DON'T RECOGNISE ME?
NO.
INCREDIBLE! SO, THE OLD WOMAN TOLD THE TRUTH.
OLD WOMAN?
SOME STRANGE OLD BIDDY I MET IN THE MOUNTAINS. SHE GAVE ME GOLD TO BUY YOU BACK FROM THE RIVER FOLK AFTER YOU KILLED ONE OF THEIR MEN.
I KILLED SOMEONE?
YES, BUT IT WAS IN OUR DEFENSE. UNFORTUNATELY, HIS PEOPLE CAPTURED YOU AND HANGED YOU BY THE FEET FROM A FRAME FOR A WHOLE DAY AND NIGHT. WITHOUT THE OLD WOMAN'S GOLD, YOU'D BE DEAD.
STRANGE... I REMEMBER NOTHING. WHO WAS THE WOMAN?
I DON'T KNOW, AND I'LL READILY ADMIT THAT I DIDN'T TRY TO UNDERSTAND. SHE JUST TOLD ME THAT YOU WERE GOING TO NEED ME, SHAIGAN. SO I RODE AS HARD AS I COULD TO SAVE YOU FROM YOUR TORTURE.
45

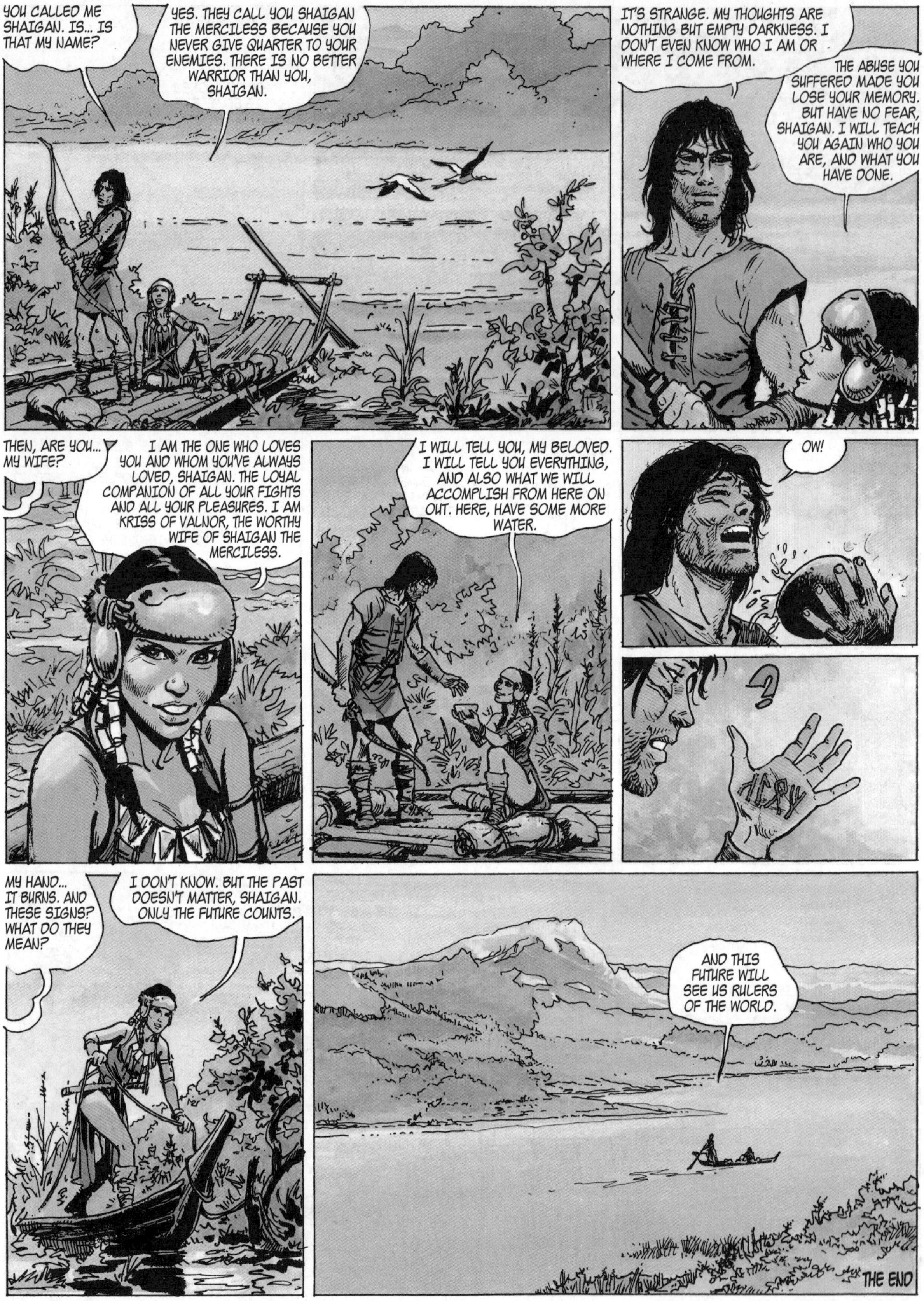
YOU CALLED ME SHAIGAN. IS... IS THAT MY NAME?
YES. THEY CALL YOU SHAIGAN THE MERCILESS BECAUSE YOU NEVER GIVE QUARTER TO YOUR ENEMIES. THERE IS NO BETTER WARRIOR THAN YOU, SHAIGAN.
IT'S STRANGE. MY THOUGHTS ARE NOTHING BUT EMPTY DARKNESS. I DON'T EVEN KNOW WHO I AM OR WHERE I COME FROM.
THE ABUSE YOU SUFFERED MADE YOU LOSE YOUR MEMORY. BUT HAVE NO FEAR, SHAIGAN. I WILL TEACH YOU AGAIN WHO YOU ARE, AND WHAT YOU HAVE DONE.
THEN, ARE YOU... MY WIFE?
I AM THE ONE WHO LOVES YOU AND WHOM YOU'VE ALWAYS LOVED, SHAIGAN. THE LOYAL COMPANION OF ALL YOUR FIGHTS AND ALL YOUR PLEASURES. I AM KRISS OF VALNOR, THE WORTHY WIFE OF SHAIGAN THE MERCILESS.
I WILL TELL YOU, MY BELOVED. I WILL TELL YOU EVERYTHING, AND ALSO WHAT WE WILL ACCOMPLISH FROM HERE ON OUT. HERE, HAVE SOME MORE WATER.
OW!
?
MY HAND... IT BURNS. AND THESE SIGNS? WHAT DO THEY MEAN?
I DON'T KNOW. BUT THE PAST DOESN'T MATTER, SHAIGAN. ONLY THE FUTURE COUNTS.
AND THIS FUTURE WILL SEE US RULERS OF THE WORLD.
THE END